puppy owner's HANDBOOK

By Jeff Griffen

STERLING PUBLISHING CO., INC. NEW YORK

Oak Tree Press Co., Ltd.
Distributed by WARD LOCK, Ltd., London & Sydney

LORD BYRON'S EPITAPH FOR HIS DOG
BURIED AT NEWSTEAD ABBEY, 1808

Near this spot
Are deposited the remains of one
Who possessed beauty without vanity,
Strength without insolence,
Courage without ferocity,
And all the virtues of man without his vices.
This praise, which would be unmeaning flattery
If inscribed over human ashes,
Is but a just tribute to the memory of
Boatswain, a dog.

Revised Edition
Copyright © 1970 by Fay MARTIN
Copyright © 1968 by Jeff GRIFFEN
Published by Sterling Publishing Co., Inc.
419 Park Avenue South, New York 10016
British edition published by Oak Tree Press Co., Ltd.
Distributed in Great Britain and the Commonwealth by
Ward Lock, Ltd., 116 Baker Street, London W1
Manufactured in the United States of America
All rights reserved
Library of Congress Catalog Card No.: 77-118327
ISBN 0-8069-3712-2   UK 7061 2246 1
3713-0

TABLE OF CONTENTS

1. YOUR NEW PUPPY 5
2. FEEDING 27
3. HOUSEBREAKING 36
4. CARE & GROOMING 43
5. HOUSING 51
6. KEEPING YOUR PUPPY HEALTHY 58
7. FIRST AID 66
8. TRAINING & TRICKS 79
9. GENERAL INFORMATION 95
10. TRAVELING WITH YOUR DOG 101
    PROFILE OF A DOG 104
    HOW YOUR DOG LEARNS 106
    INDEX 107

Lift your puppy correctly by holding one hand under his bottom and another against his chest.

1

YOUR NEW PUPPY

Congratulations!

You have bought a sound, healthy, reliable pal who will bring you many years of loyal companionship and happiness. All that the puppy asks in return is tender loving care, which is fair enough because it is completely dependent upon you for its needs. We're going to tell you the basic information you should know about its care and all we ask is that you follow the suggestions.

When you first bring your puppy home, it may lose its playfulness momentarily because of the strange sounds, sights and people, but this will return just as soon as it becomes settled in its new surroundings. Don't put the puppy on your brand-new rug or carpet; it may piddle out of excitement. Have patience, give it love and encouragement, and above all, don't let excited children come screaming up and maul it. Also, if you have another dog, don't put the puppy down in front of him. The old-timer may be jealous and resent the intrusion. Introduce them gradually.

The first thing to learn is how to lift your puppy correctly. Don't hoist him by the front legs as it can easily injure him. Don't lift him by the scruff of the neck or use his tail as a handle either. Place one hand under his chest and the other under his stomach and raise him gently.

Be sure to teach children how to handle the puppy properly, and under no circumstances let small tots lift the puppy. They may accidentally drop it and cause serious injury. Be careful they don't sit on it also. Children must be taught to handle and treat the puppy with kindness. No pulling of ears or tail, no sticking fingers in eyes or mouth, and especially no teasing or chasing the puppy.

It will pay you to watch the puppy in the beginning so it doesn't get into such mischief as chewing or pulling on things in fun. Which brings us to the second point. When do you start training your puppy? The answer is—the moment you get it. Remember that when you bought your puppy, you didn't buy a problem and it won't be one unless you make it into one. Your puppy will respond according to your display of pleasure or displeasure, so start showing it right away. The learning situation always involves tension. Response in the form of a harsh-sounding voice, a threatening gesture, a shaking by the collar or a spanking increases the tension. Response such as a pat on the side, a happy tone of voice or a tidbit reward creates confidence and leads the puppy in that direction. Your puppy's instinctive desire to please urges him to seek the reward of

Have a wire crate or playpen in which to enclose your puppy at night.

your good graces. He tries to do what you want, and thus he learns! Let this whole process begin at once.

Here are some important points to remember:

The biggest dangers to puppies are drafts, stairways and other dogs. Drafts lead to colds, which lead to more serious problems. Puppies unknowingly tumble down stairs and break bones. Other healthy-looking dogs can carry diseases, so keep your puppy away from them until he has had protective shots.

Arrange a sleeping place for your puppy that will be exclusively his. The best thing you can do for yourself and your puppy is to have a crate or box in which you can close up your puppy at night. This makes housebreaking much easier, as we will explain later; it also acts as a place of security which the dog soon grows to love, and it eliminates all kinds of problems when you leave the dog alone. If you wish to change to an open basket at a later time, you can easily do so; but in the beginning use a wire or wooden crate that has a good solid latch. Depending upon whether you have a small, medium or large dog, be sure to buy or make a crate large enough for him to grow in.

If you use a wire crate and put it near an open window, place a towel or light blanket over the crate's top and sides for protection, but leave the front open for air.

Prepare a place for the puppy to run the following morning, because as soon as he gets out of the crate he will have to relieve himself. Cover the area with newspapers spread two or three pages thick. Spray a small circle of housebreak trainer on the paper which will attract the puppy to the area you want him to use.

If, during the night, your puppy cries a little, don't coddle or baby him. It will only make him worse. Tell him, "Quiet!" in a firm voice and put a loud, ticking clock beside his crate, or a radio turned on low with soft music.

Your puppy is most likely to relieve himself right after a meal, when he first gets out of his crate in the morning, or if he is frightened. The usual indication is sniffing, then turning round and round a couple of times, then squatting, so be prepared for these signals.

Find a veterinarian, either by looking in the phone book or asking a friend who owns a dog. Make an appointment and take your puppy to him for a health inspection and for permanent shots. Be sure to do this within 5 days after purchase so that if you have a guarantee it can be activated. Have the veterinarian fill out the back of the guarantee. This is done for your protection and your dog's health. Don't neglect it!

Establish a working relationship with your veterinarian so that you can go to him in an emergency or whenever his help is needed. You will have the added advantage of his wide knowledge on almost every phase of your dog's life. Often just a phone call will be enough.

A word here on inoculations. They are absolutely imperative for your dog whether you live in the city, suburbia or rural area. Most states have laws requiring a rabies shot every year for public-safety reasons. In addition, your veterinarian will inoculate the puppy for protection against distemper, hepatitis and leptospirosis, which are very serious canine diseases but not communicable to people. These deadly viruses are transmitted by other dogs, by people's clothing, and even through the air. An annual booster shot will help protect your dog from these difficult-to-cure diseases.

Another point to remember is that a puppy's bones are soft, his joints, tendons and leg muscles undeveloped, so don't allow him to jump off high places like chairs, beds and sofas, particularly if he is toy size. Also, he has a soft spot on the top of his head which makes him highly vulnerable to blows in that area.

Puppies are famous for three things—playing, sleeping and eating.

No tug-of-war or roughhousing.

A puppy at play is a most heartwarming sight, whether he is chasing his tail or scampering after a ball or licking a child's face. There are some rules to the game however. Don't let the young puppy 8 to 12 weeks of age overexercise to the point of exhaustion. Children want to play and play with the little puppy until it can't stand up. Fifteen or 20 minutes at a time is enough. Let the puppy lie down and rest then.

No roughhousing with your puppy. This can lead to all sorts of bad habits, including nipping. What invariably happens in roughhousing is that the puppy soon learns to defend himself, and the more a child or adult pushes the puppy into this situation, the more he resorts to biting. No playing tug-of-war either. This is bad for the dog's teeth and soon teaches him to pull on anything he can get hold of—the dining table cloth, the hems on women's dresses, the drapes. All of this seems funny at first, but when it gets out of hand and you have to chastise the dog, the poor animal can't understand it, since you encouraged him to do it before. This is exactly why we say that most of the misdemeanors committed by your dog will be of your own making by allowing or encouraging him to do the wrong thing.

Encourage your puppy to play constructively. Let him retrieve a ball; this will teach him his name and to come when called. Take him for short walks on his leash or let him play with a squeaker toy. You will find all kinds, shapes and sizes at your pet shop, and toys are necessary playthings for your pet.

If you find your puppy chews up his toys, get him a leather bone or some leather discs to chew on. Never give him an old shoe because he will only think that shoes are for the purpose of being chewed up. The leather bones sold by pet shops are pacifiers and will be particularly helpful when the dog begins to teethe at 4 or 5 months of age.

Some puppies want to chew more than others and it is sometimes difficult to train them out of the desire. A better way is to give them a harmless, tasty diversion to chew on and admonish them when they start on something they shouldn't, like a table leg, chair fringe or electric light cord.

In the event that chewing persists, simply get a can of what is called "chewcheck" and spray it on furniture or any object that the puppy gnaws on. Its bitter, unpleasant flavor will cause him to avoid further munching, and normally only one or two applications are necessary.

Also, if you have fine furniture that you don't want your puppy to sleep on—a Louis Quinze sofa or Martha Washington armchair, etc.— buy a can of dog repellent. This cures your dog of sleeping or resting

Be sure to select the proper collar and leash for your puppy.

on forbidden objects and in unwanted areas of the home. Follow the directions on the can carefully so that the fabric is not harmed.

A puppy needs lots of sleep. After a spell of playing or after finishing a meal, he will want to lie down and snooze. This is fine, and he should be encouraged to do so. No playing right after meals though; the exercise may cause him to vomit. Let him rest instead. If you have a particularly active puppy, take him for a walk just before going to bed. It will help him to sleep better through the entire night.

Don't encourage your puppy to jump on you, especially if he is a large breed. No dog should be allowed to jump on you or your guests. It is not only annoying but can ruin stockings and soil clothes. The proper thing is to bend over and reach your puppy's level. He won't have to jump then and he'll be much happier because it's a long way up from his level to yours. Also, bending over to hug him or pat him or greet him tends to calm and reassure him and avoids the bouncing, yo-yo type of attitude that so easily develops.

Feeding your puppy is covered thoroughly in the next chapter. Suffice it to say here that you should have a pan for food and a pan for water. Don't use dishes as they overturn too easily. Get the no-tip kind with the wide flat bottom in either stainless steel or plastic.

You also want a collar and leash. Don't leave the store without buying these, otherwise you'll have no way to control your puppy. There are many kinds of collars to choose from—leather, chain, nylon, plain and fancy. A leather one is best in the beginning. The small, toy breeds do best on a rolled collar; so do the long-haired breeds because a rolled collar will not wear away hair or become entangled in it. Medium and large dogs should have flat leather collars. Let the pet shop manager help you select the proper size. Later on, especially if you have a medium or large-sized breed, you will want a chain collar for training.

As for a leash, you should have at least two: one a 4- to 6-foot leash for walking and training, the other a 12- to 15-foot web type which will give your dog a little more freedom when you want to do so. If you have a large dog in the city, it is also practical to have a traffic leash which comes 12- to 18-inches long and gives you thorough control over your dog at all times.

The first time you put the collar on your puppy he will probably go through all kinds of jumping contortions in an effort to get it off his neck. Just leave it on, reassure him a little, and in no time at all he will have forgotten about it. In the large, fast-growing breeds, be sure to check the collar frequently to make certain it's not too tight on the dog's neck. It should be snug enough so as not to slip over the head, but not tight

If your puppy balks, coax and praise him until he follows you.

enough to choke him. An occasional one-notch expansion as the puppy grows will keep the collar at its proper adjustment. A rule of thumb is to place two fingers side-by-side under the collar to determine proper fit.

A few days after the puppy has gotten accustomed to his collar, you should try leading him a bit with the leash. This will be the first time he has been made to do something he has not chosen to do. Let him drag the leash around the living room for two or three minutes several times, then try leading him. If he balks, praise him, coax him to follow you. Make your pressure a slow steady pull, not a jerk. Let up when the puppy begins to come along and praise him with your voice, even with some happy hand clapping.

Another way is to put him in the middle of the living room or outdoors on the lawn and follow him as he begins to walk about. This is particularly effective if he is a very young puppy, 7 to 12 weeks old. By the time he is 16 weeks of age, he will have developed enough physically and mentally to grasp quickly what is wanted. The younger you start at this leash training, the better your results will be in this and all other training. Science has proven that the more you teach the dog at a young age the easier it is for him to learn later. Respect for you and the learning habit become part of his life, and he matures into a happy, well-balanced dog who is a pleasure to have around.

Another important facet that dog authorities strongly recommend is "affection training" or "socializing." This means *getting your dog out into the world at a young age so he adjusts properly to his surroundings.* We cannot overstress the importance of teaching your puppy to ride in a car, go up and down stairs and elevators, to be friendly in the presence of other people and dogs. This "socializing" should begin the moment your puppy has had his permanent shots. The purpose is to give your dog an outgoing, well-adjusted personality. It is done by your taking him out into the world at every opportunity while he is under 6 months of age. When you go shopping or marketing, take him with you. Get him accustomed to people, sounds, smells, whistles, trains, and buses.

If you leave him home constantly in his early life, he will become inhibited, hide under the couch when guests come or be overly protective of his domain. Even if you bought your dog for protection purposes, you don't want him to have a shy or inhibited personality.

If you wish your dog to safeguard your home, bring him up as healthily as possible, teach him to bark on command as we will show you later, and let him stay in the car when you go shopping. His protective instincts will develop naturally and to a sufficient degree that you need do little else for him to serve you well in this regard.

Take your dog out into the world at every opportunity.

    As they mature, and depending upon the breed, dogs instinctively grow protective of their master and home. They do it by barking at strangers or unexpected sounds, growling if provoked. Large dogs have the habit of standing between their master and strangers. Under no condition do you want to develop your pet into an attack dog. He may charge the wrong person—a friend or child who innocently does something.

Never let a child sneak up and startle your dog while it is sleeping. The animal's instincts are self-protective and the child may come off with more than he expected.

If you keep your dog indoors, you may want some kind of sweater for it when you take it walking. This is particularly true of the smaller, short-haired breeds who, coming from the heated interior of home, feel the cold much more. Your pet shop probably has several models and sizes, simple or elaborate, for your dog. It is wise to use one in winter when chilling winds with freezing temperatures and snow are frequent. If your dog becomes overly chilled when he goes outside for a walk, it is not only bad for him physically but he is less inclined to do his duties as he normally would, consequently he is more liable to have an accident in the house or apartment.

Same on rainy days. Your dog needs a raincoat just as you do when he goes outside in inclement weather. The raincoat not only protects him but keeps his coat dry so that when he returns home he will not immediately shake himself to free his coat of water. Of course, it's not necessary for retrievers who have almost waterproof double-coats, or for other long-haired breeds.

For toy dogs there are cute little umbrella leashes which can be used and look very attractive when walking your pet on a rainy city street.

Whenever you return from a walk in slushy, damp or rainy weather, it is wise to have a bath towel handy to wipe off the dog's feet. It only takes a moment and keeps the carpet or rugs from being soiled. In fact, many people wipe their dog's feet off after every outing. It not only helps to eliminate foot prints but reduces the chances of disease immensely because dogs, in the natural process of cleaning themselves, lick the bottoms of their feet and can contract all kinds of viruses picked up from the street or gutter. There are also dog boots that are fine for walking in the rain and especially in slush and snow.

Your puppy needs fresh air and sunshine, not quantities of the broiling kind of hot summer sun. This might give him a heat stroke. But he should have a reasonable amount of sunlight daily either inside or outside. Outside housing will be covered more thoroughly later. If you keep your puppy inside, it is helpful to have a play pen into which you can put him while getting supper or doing the house cleaning. In that way he is out from under your feet so you can't step on him inadvertently, also he is out of mischief.

If you don't have a play pen, use some sort of fence or extension gate. The kind that is used for children serves well for big dogs, but small ones can squeeze through it. A piece of hardware wire on a frame works well.

As a last resort, you can tie the puppy to a radiator or some other object, but he should not be left there for any length of time.

Whenever you place your puppy in a play pen or tie him, be sure to provide something for him to play with, preferably a leather bone. Also, place his mat nearby so he can lie on it. Dogs are creatures of habit and if you start with a puppy and train him to lie on his mat, he will do so all his life no matter where you go. When you check into a motel or visit a friend for a weekend, you can simply drop his sleeping mat in a convenient corner and say, "Lie down!" or "Kennel!" and the dog will feel perfectly at home lying on the object that he knows is his.

Some people tend to make their dog so dependent upon them that when they leave the animal for any reason, it becomes so infuriated that it tears up clothing, furniture, pillows, all sorts of things. The way to stop this is to prevent it from starting. Your wire cage, mentioned earlier, or play pen comes in handy here. You want to take the puppy as many places as possible while it is young, but you must also teach it to be contented by itself when the occasion necessitates. The thing to do is take your puppy shopping with you one day so it learns to go out into life and activity happily, then leave it home the next day so it learns that there are times when it will be alone. Be sure to practice both of these.

Disciplining your puppy properly is another important phase of his upbringing. Like everything else, there is a right and a wrong way. Never strike him in anger, and never punish him for something he did five minutes before. *You must catch him in the act; otherwise don't punish him.* For example, if your dog fails to come when you call him, don't spank him when he finally does. He will only think that you are punishing him for coming and will be worse than ever.

You should teach your puppy the command of "No!" at an early age. This is something that you will use throughout his life to restrain him or make him stop whatever he is doing. Say it in a loud sharp voice, at the same time holding the puppy firmly by the collar so he has to look at you, and shake your finger in his face.

As the puppy grows older and more willful, roll up a few sheets of newspaper and use it to slap the side of your leg or top of a table when you see him making a mistake. The sharp crack of sound will gain his attention; then you can say "No!"

Most of your early disciplining will be in the housebreaking and chewing areas. If your puppy starts to piddle accidentally on the floor, never strike him with the rolled-up newspaper but hit the floor beside him. Immediately snatch him up and put him on the paper where you want him to go. Also be sure to clean up the spot thoroughly afterwards. Pet shops

Wipe off puppy's feet after he comes in.

Teach your puppy the command "No!" at an early age. You will use this command all his life.

have an excellent stain remover that also destroys the odor so the puppy won't be attracted to the place again. Use it and save yourself a lot of headaches, for your puppy will inevitably make an occasional mistake.

A point you should be careful about. If you have an exuberant dog who is enormously glad to see you when you return home—to the extent of bouncing up and down, barking, and mouthing your hand—be sure you bend over and calm him down. This merely means standing still and holding the dog still and letting him lick your face while you say, "Yes, yes, old pal. Okay, okay."

Above all, discourage any mouthing of your hand even if you have to tap the dog across the muzzle with a forefinger and say a firm, "No!" Or even better, you can thrust your palm sharply against his nose, not hard enough to hurt him but enough to dispel this potentially bad habit right in the beginning. As the dog grows older, his tendency will be to play harder until the day comes that he won't let go easily. Then some youngster is liable to become frightened, smack the dog in the face, and you have the makings of trouble.

A dog should be introduced to people just as other people are, particularly in the case of a puppy. This teaches the puppy not to be shy in the presence of strangers and to accept other people into his home without any undue fuss. This does not mean that he will wag his tail at prowlers who come stealing around. Indeed, his hair will bristle, and he will immediately suspect the intruder. Dogs almost invariably know the difference between friend and foe around the home. It merely means that he will be happy among your guests as he should be.

Teach the tiny puppy to come when called, by tidbits and clapping your hands.

There are doggy britches and odor-ending pills for your female when she comes into season.

If yours is one of the giant or more protective breeds, some of your friends will be concerned about entering at first. To allay all fears, you should introduce them to the dog as well as the dog to them. Children should also be introduced to the dog and told to treat it kindly. When approaching the dog, they should extend the back of their hand in a gentle manner and let the dog sniff it. A child should never be allowed to run up to a strange dog and, screaming in glee, throw his arms around the pet's neck. In meeting a strange dog for the first time, one should not pat the top of the dog's head. The downward gesture often creates sudden fear. It is much better to scratch the dog's ear or rub its throat gently, both of which bring pleasure to the dog.

Now that you have a puppy you should get a small medicine chest or put aside a certain shelf in a cabinet for the handy, practical things. You won't need many things but, in the event of sickness or emergency, they will prove invaluable. Right now, all you need are a small jar of vaseline, a thermometer for taking your puppy's temperature rectally, and a package of cotton balls. Later, we will tell you other things to add. Be sure to label any medicine given you by the veterinarian. Write on the tube or jar exactly what it is for—"For Eyes," "For Ears," "For Skin," or whatever. Thus you will never mix the medicines and accidentally put something for the ears in the dog's eyes.

Be sure to teach your puppy his name just as soon as possible. Use it when playing with him or calling him. Have a little tidbit reward in the form of a "Treat." Call him by name while you are on hands and knees, and give him a taste when he responds properly. These little "Treats" are like candy for your puppy and, besides containing vitamins, they make excellent training rewards.

When you pick a name for your puppy, you should actually choose two—the one which will appear on his registration papers and the one which will serve as his call name. The one that appears on his pedigree and is registered with the American Kennel Club is always a fancy, high-toned, three- or four-word monicker such as *Sir Launcelot of Central Park* or *Great Oaks White Lady*. Often it includes the kennel name of the breeder.

But the call name you use for your dog should be simple and no more than one or two syllables. You don't want a tongue twister when you go to call your dog. And you don't want a name that rhymes with a command that you will be using later, such as *Joe* and *No*! This will only tend to confuse the dog.

Your puppy will grow very rapidly the first 7 or 8 months of his life, particularly if he is of a larger breed. Here is the pattern you can expect your puppy to follow.

At 3 months he will be quarter grown, full of fun, play and mischievousness, still wobble-legged and dependent upon you for his confidence.

At 6 months he will be half grown, surer-footed, stronger, sharp as a tack in his intelligence and awareness of surroundings, eating all the food he can find, growing like a weed and always on the go-go-go.

At 8 to 10 months he will be three-quarters grown, rather ungainly and not quite co-ordinated but full of enthusiasm, the puppy manners replaced by more independence and willfulness.

At 11 to 13 months he will reach his full height, needing only to fill out in muscles and rib cage to be an adult dog. He will possess a mind of his own and be essentially whatever he is going to be.

During your puppy's first year of life, many changes will take place in him.

At 4 to 5 months of age he will lose his baby or milk teeth. This sore process may momentarily change his personality. His gums will grow red and inflamed, he may become grouchy, want to chew on things more than usual or stop eating altogether. When you look at his mouth you will see that the sharp little baby teeth are loose or coming out. Sometimes the buds of the new ones will be showing beside them.

If the baby teeth are loose enough to remove with your fingers, it will be helpful to do so. Simply lay the puppy on his side, have someone hold his head and shoulders so he doesn't wriggle too much. Talk to him soothingly while at the same time slipping your fingers into his mouth. You will be able to pull them out with a quick little jerk so he never knows it. If one seems to be blocking the entrance of a permanent tooth, it is wise to take the puppy to a veterinarian and have him extract it. Pulling the puppy's teeth the moment they loosen will make the permanent ones come in straight.

If you have a female puppy, her first season or menstrual period will begin at around 8 to 10 months of age, occasionally earlier, sometimes later, and lasting 3 weeks. Every 6 months thereafter she will have another. At these times only, she will be capable of being bred and attract male dogs to her by a body scent in her urine. Science has now found a way to eliminate this odor and such pills (entirely harmless) are available at your favorite pet shop. Nevertheless, the bitch must be carefully isolated, for Nature compels her to all sorts of effort to meet a mate. Owners often send their dogs to a boarding kennel during this time.

First signs of approach of the season are a swelling of the vulva and a

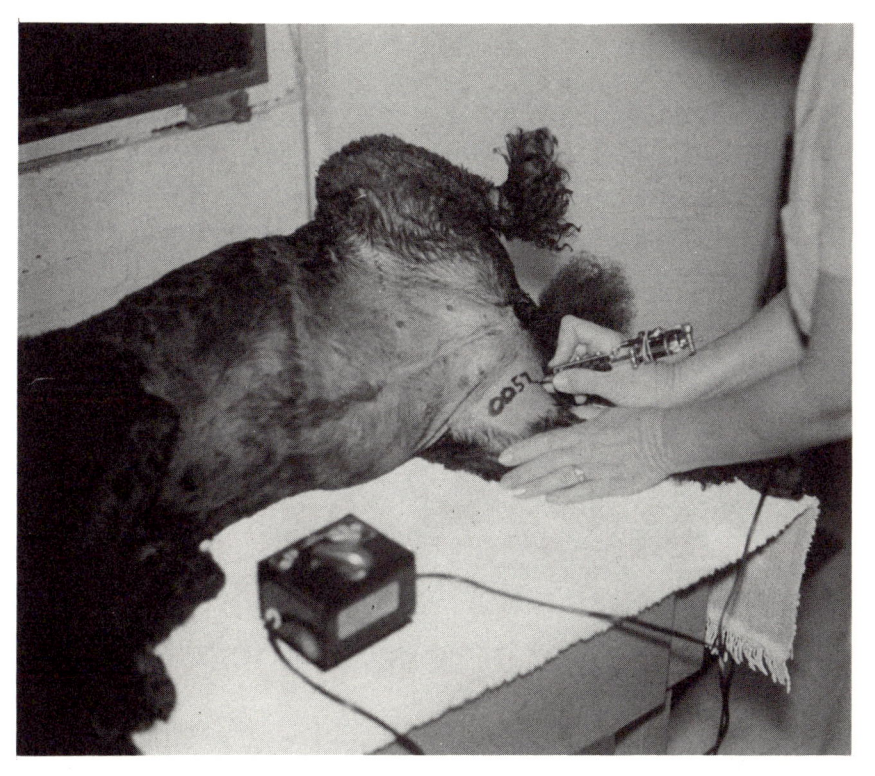

Tattoo your dog for positive identification and help against theft.

bloody discharge which will be messy around your home unless you keep her clean. You can buy what are called "petite panties" which will be most helpful. Don't let the female run loose. She must be hand-exercised. In the event that an accidental mating occurs, take her to your veterinarian immediately. He may be able to prevent conception.

If you wish to breed your female, the proper time is during the second week, usually between the tenth and thirteenth day. But she should be at least 18 months old before this is done.

Many owners save themselves the trouble and expense of isolation by having the female spayed. The operation, most easily performed at 5 to 7 months of age, eliminates all the fuss and bother. If properly fed and exercised, the female does not become excessively fat, nor is her disposition or alertness impaired. Afterwards, the female can never have puppies and is ineligible for bench shows though she may still enter

Height of a dog is from floor to shoulders.

obedience competition, but the advantages far outweigh the disadvantages if she is to be a good house pet, companion or watchdog.

The male dog can be castrated without any undue problems and again the advantages are favorable unless you wish to show or breed him. He becomes more docile and manageable, more devoted to the family and much cleaner in his toilet habits. Speak to your veterinarian about the possibility of this.

During the growing-up period of the first year, both male and female dogs sometimes develop the objectionable habit of mounting one's leg or another animal. This should be discouraged immediately, and the dog made to understand in no uncertain terms that it will not be tolerated. If not checked in the beginning, it can be embarrassing to guests and annoying to children.

Later in the first year of the puppy's life, usually between the eighth and eleventh month, the dog will shed its puppy coat and get its permanent one. A slight change in color will occur in some breeds at this time. The coat change does not affect the health of the dog in any way, but the more healthy your dog is, the better his coat will be. A vitamin supplement added to the food at this time, particularly one with an amino acid base, will be helpful. You will find several excellent ones at your nearby pet shop or store. In the event that your dog, either as a puppy or an adult, seems to shed unduly, speak to your veterinarian. There are several possible causes of it—a deficient diet, worms, skin ailments. He can quickly isolate the trouble and help cure it.

Within the first year of your puppy's life, the law in most states requires that you license your dog. Usually this is at 6 months of age but it varies. Be sure to check in your locality and see when this is necessary. A license allows you to harbor your dog but does not serve as positive legal identification.

The only type of permanent identification for your dog is tattooing. In recent years, dog thefts have soared to over half a million annually in the U.S. The stolen dogs are sold to research labs by unscrupulous dealers. Federal laws have tried to prohibit this traffic to the extent that any laboratory or medical school now rejects any dog that is tattooed. There are at least three national registries for this, and if you value your pet, it will be a worthwhile investment that costs very little. Your veterinarian can give you more particulars and do the tattooing for you, either in the groin or in the ear.

Here are a few facts that you should know about **dogs in general**:

The female is correctly referred to as a bitch. A brood bitch is a female used primarily for breeding.

The male is correctly called a dog. A stud dog is a male used primarily for breeding.

The period of gestation for dogs is 58 to 65 days, averaging 63.

The height of a dog is determined by a measurement from the ground to the top of his shoulders.

Each breed of dog has an official *Standard* which is a description of what the dog should look like. A copy of this may be obtained from the American Kennel Club, 51 Madison Avenue, New York, N.Y.

Almost every breed of dog has a national club and several local clubs scattered throughout the country. The American Kennel Club, upon request, will inform you of the club nearest you.

Let's move on now, to other important phases of your puppy.

>
> 'Tis sweet to hear the watch-dog's honest bark
> Bay deep-mouth'd welcome as we draw near home;
> 'Tis sweet to know there is an eye will mark
> Our coming, and look brighter when we come.
>
> —*Lord Byron*

2
FEEDING

If the right breed of dog is matched to the right family situation, many problems are solved before they ever start.

Carrying this same idea over into the feeding of your dog, we shall tell you how you can feed your dog in the least amount of time and yet have the best results. We say this because in this day and age, time is important. Most dog owners, whether it be a family with school kids, a working girl or man, are busy, active people who must budget their hours. We would rather see you take the time required to buy, cook and prepare elaborate home-made meals and use it to enjoy your dog, go for a walk with him or train him better.

If you want to pamper your dog with fancy meals, go right ahead. It isn't necessary, so we recommend a system designed for people on the go and who still want to own a dog and enjoy all the laughs and companionship that man's best friend has to offer.

Basically there are three ways to feed your dog:

1. You can prepare your dog's diet from human food and leftovers which, unless you are a nutritionist, is the poorest way of all and usually results in the dog being fed only the things that he likes.
2. You can mix a feeding of commercial dog food of the dry, semi-moist or canned (if it is "complete") type.
3. You can put commercially prepared, nutritionally complete, dog foods in front of him and leave them there for him to nibble on whenever he gets hungry.

The first two systems require that you feed the growing puppy 3 to 5 times a day, which means that you must be present to do it.

The second system requires only that you keep dry food and water available for the puppy, which means you have little or no bother at all but your puppy suffers somewhat for your companionship.

The third system requires only that you keep dry food and water and is as ideal a method as you can use. It requires that you feed the growing puppy only twice a day, breakfast and supper, when you would normally be there; the rest of the time, dry food is left for him to consume during the day whenever he desires it. Simple and practical for you, nutritional for him.

Suppose you get home a little late from work... no problem because the puppy has food available to nibble on if he wants it. Even if you don't get home until midnight, your puppy still has food and water.

Furthermore, unless you're a professional nutritionist, you can't prepare a better balanced diet than most of the ready-made ones put out by major dog food companies. They have spent millions of dollars in research and the U.S. Department of Agriculture has set up a level of minimum daily requirements for dogs. The result is that most dogs in the United States, when fed commercially prepared, nutritionally complete, dog food, have better diets than many of our citizens who try to survive on soda pop and ice cream cones.

When you buy your puppy, at 8 to 10 weeks of age or older, find out if he has been on a special diet. Be familiar with that diet and if you change from it, the transition should be gradual. Thus your puppy will eat well from the start and there will be no problem of changing from one food to another. His diet should consist of any good puppy kibble or meal with a little cooked or canned meat added for flavor, also a small amount of water for moistening. Let the kibble absorb water for 3 or 4 minutes, then feed immediately to the puppy.

You will feed your puppy, regardless of age, a morning and evening meal consisting of the above simple-to-prepare diet. The rest of the time you will place a container of the same dry kibble beside the puppy's water bowl and let him eat as he wishes, when he wishes.

If you want to add any vitamins or special supplements to his diet, you can simply stir them into one of the meals which you prepare.

If you have table scraps left over—vegetables, rice, gravy, any kind of meat, even bits of fat—they can be added to the canned or cooked meat.

Two important points to remember:

Be sure the kibble or meal which you buy says on the package, "This is a Complete Diet" or words to that effect. "Complete" in this sense means all the required vitamins and minerals, protein and other elements, are included.

Never add more than 25% of cooked or canned meat or table scraps to the kibble or meal. As long as you keep at least a 75% kibble or meal base, you will not upset the balance of the diet.

To feed your puppy if you have to go to work, leave dry food and water for him.

Once again, the feeding formula is: Kibble or meal plus cooked or canned meat or table scraps in 75–25% ratio, with water enough to moisten.

The cooked meat we speak of is horse meat or beef. Cook it with some water just a few minutes so the meat is still on the rare side and juicy. Use the broth instead of water when mixing with the dry food. The cheapest grade of hamburger is also excellent because it contains some fat which is helpful to all dogs and should be included in the diet. You can buy the basic kibble or meal, along with the fresh, frozen or canned meat at any supermarket.

Some companies put out a special puppy kibble or meal which is excellent and slightly more nourishing than the regular dry food. Also, you

Never add more than 25% of cooked or canned meat or table scraps to kibble or meal.

can feed the semi-moist "burgers" during the day if you find your dog isn't eating the dry food very well. These prepared patties, also available in supermarkets, are highly nutritious and very palatable food for him.

How much do you feed your dog?

This depends upon the size, but a growing puppy, like a growing boy, eats more than an adult proportionally. A toy-sized puppy has a stomach

Don't overfeed the large breed of puppy during first year.

no larger than a golf ball, so don't be concerned if he doesn't gorge himself. On the other hand, a full-grown Irish Wolfhound will eat two or three pounds per meal. Determine the right amount for your dog by experimenting a little. Use a cup to measure the meal. If he is a toy like a Yorkshire Terrier, try half a cup; a small dog like a Cocker, one cup; medium-sized dog like a Dalmatian, two cups; large dog like a standard Poodle, 3 cups; extra-large like a Great Dane, 4 cups. This amount will be fed twice a day. Because nutritional values vary with different brands of dog food, be sure to follow the directions on the label.

An active, well-exercised dog or one with considerable nervous energy will burn up more food than the dog with quiet habits. Watch your

31

puppy's weight. If he is well filled out and has trouble finishing the last bit of food, cut down a little. If he is forever hungry, growing fast and eats all his dry food each day, give him more.

Naturally, as the puppy grows, you will have to increase the food intake, but don't leave any unfinished meal before him longer than 10 minutes. If he occasionally skips a meal entirely, don't be concerned. Only when he goes off his food for a day or two should you call your veterinarian for help. Always take his temperature first.

One thing we must stress here is not to overfeed if you have a large or very large dog. Although the plump butterball puppy may look cute, you may easily create problems for him by keeping him too fat. If his body weight becomes more than his young, undeveloped bone structure can handle during the first 6 months of his life, permanent damage can result. We strongly recommend that large breeds such as Golden Retrievers and German Shepherds, and extra-large breeds like St. Bernards and Great Danes not be overfed but kept on the lean side until they are 6 months old and their bone structure well formed.

No dog should ever be allowed to get too fat or obese at any stage in its life. It is not healthy. Some dogs, like some people, put on weight easily, while others can eat all day and never gain an ounce.

The feeding pattern described above can be continued for the entire first year. After that, the mature dog does not normally require as much food, so you can eliminate one meal, most likely breakfast. Keep the dry food available for him during the day, however.

Always be sure to have water available beside the dry food. This is important. Fresh water, cool or at room temperature, should be available at all times anyway.

As for supplements to be added to your puppy's food, there are all kinds and descriptions. Calcium and bone meal help supply the demands of fast growing bone structures in large and extra large dogs. Wheat germ oil helps the coats of all dogs; cod liver oil helps provide vitamins A and C. Some dogs require vitamins, others do not. Your veterinarian can tell by looking at the conformation and physical makeup of your dog whether it needs supplements. Speak to him about it and be guided by his advice.

Twice a week it is an excellent idea to put a tablespoon of bacon grease or margarine in the puppy's food. Fat is one element that cannot be stored in commercial dog foods in sufficient quantities. Including some occasionally in the dog's diet adds to his general health.

In buying commercial dog food, be sure to buy the best you can get since this is the foundation of your dog's diet and whatever else you add is mainly for palatability.

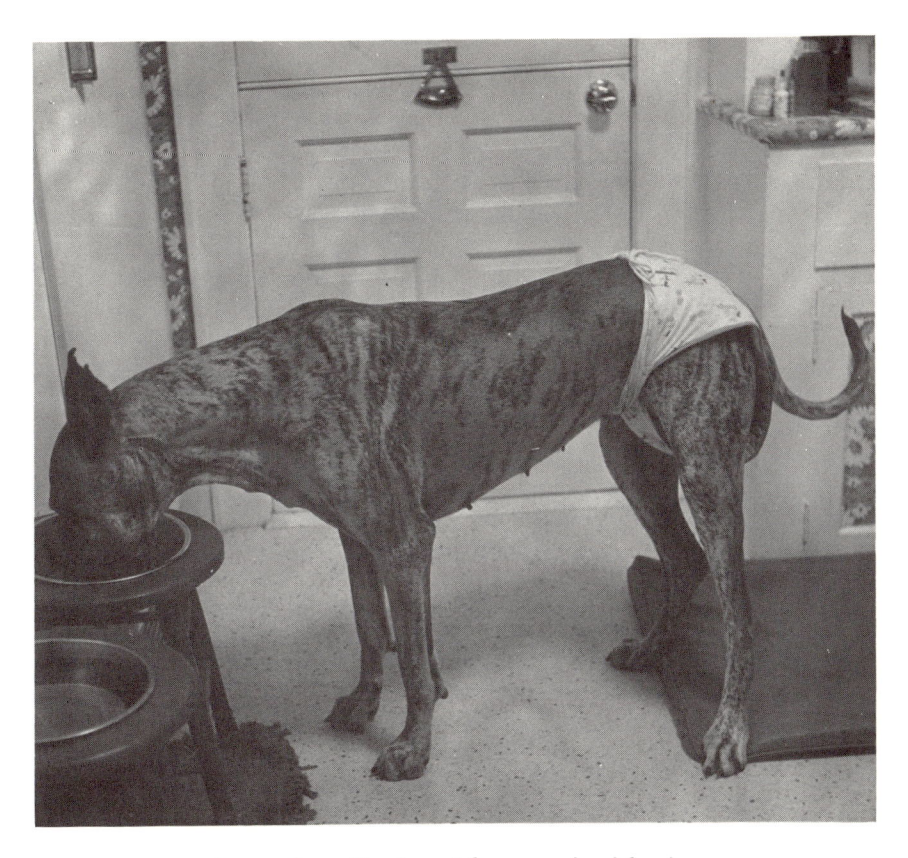

Large dogs like to eat from a raised feeder.

By nature, all dogs love bones, but there are two problems in feeding them. First, certain types of bones like pork chop, lamb chop and some beef bones will splinter and be so sharp when the dog swallows them that they can punch holes in the stomach wall or intestines. Also, as any veterinarian will tell you, it is not uncommon to have a dog gorge himself on bones to the extent that he develops a stoppage in the intestine and dies. Bones are better off not fed to your dog, but if you feel you must do so, make them large shin bones or knuckle bones that he can gnaw on but cannot break up and swallow. You can buy prepared bones for dogs that are like chewing pacifiers. These will not splinter and satisfy your dog's yearning for bones. Never feed him chop bones, poultry or fish bones.

Very large dogs often eat better when they don't have to bend way over to reach their food. A handy feeder as shown in the photo can be used. It is made by cutting a hole in the top of a stool large enough to hold the pan. Medium-sized and small dogs also enjoy the convenience of comfortable eating.

The adult dog can live on a wide variety of diets, but many of these will not keep him in the best of health. His coat will show the effects, as will his teeth and other organs. A poor diet can even shorten his life, so make every attempt to feed your dog a good sound diet.

Here are some additional feeding tips you should know about:

Canned meat is not a complete diet regardless of what the advertising may imply. It is the most palatable of all dog foods but, if fed as a constant diet, could lead to malnutrition.

Many dogs show a liking for bizarre foods such as fresh fruits, raw vegetables, nuts, candies, etc. Unusual items are not harmful if fed only once in a while, but don't let them interfere with regular feedings.

There is nothing wrong with giving your dog a snack at bedtime. A biscuit or cracker or small bowl of milk will please him while you raid the refrigerator.

Some dogs, as they grow older, develop considerable amount of gas, the passing of which can be annoying to those around him. Feeding a charcoal biscuit once a day will usually minimize or eliminate the problem.

It is not true that "milk makes worms" or that "feeding raw meat will make a dog vicious." Nor will "garlic or raw onions kill worms in a dog." Raw eggs are not good for a dog either. Yolks may be fed raw, but the uncooked whites destroy vitamins. Whole eggs should be cooked if they are to be fed to a dog.

Don't be concerned if your puppy or adult dog bolts down his food. It's normal for a dog to eat fast and swallow his food whole. The various facets of his digestive processes will break down the food for digestion later.

Dogs can digest and utilize starchy foods like potatoes and macaroni or bread, but a steady diet of starch is not healthy. Rice is an excellent food, particularly when a dog has loose bowels. It is best boiled with a little meat to make it more tasty.

Again, water is of prime importance to a dog in winter and summer. Your dog has no skin pores through which he can perspire; his only way is through the saliva glands in his mouth, which is why he pants when hot. Water, as we have often repeated, should be available at all times.

As your dog grows elderly, he may become thin and his coat harsh and dry. To obtain the full benefit of his food you may need to feed him twice a day; smaller amounts at each feeding are easier on the digestive system. You may want to add some high potency vitamins, but it is best to consult

Many dogs like bizarre food. This is a sweet pickle.

your veterinarian about this. An old dog is particularly sensitive to change. A new feeding dish or a different person preparing the food may cause him to skip a meal, but patience and tender loving care soon bring him back to normal again.

Don't let feeding be a chore. Keep it simple as we have outlined, and you will have a happy healthy dog.

3
HOUSEBREAKING

Your dog is a very clean animal by nature. This is the key to housebreaking him. It's not nearly so difficult a chore as it sounds, and once accomplished, it is done for life. The older the dog gets, the more understanding he becomes and will, in time, approach you to ask to go out. The process is not so much teaching your dog to be clean as it is giving him a chance to stay clean.

Housebreaking is accomplished in two steps. The first is paper training which prepares the way for the second, that of having your puppy go outside to relieve himself.

At what age does housebreaking start?

Like all training, just as soon as you get your puppy.

The first step—paper training—is a must for all apartment dogs. They should be taught to go on paper first, then to go outside later. Going outside either by elevator or down the stairs is sometimes confusing to a dog, hence the step from paper training to housebreaking for the city dog often takes longer.

For house dogs in suburbia, paper training is helpful but not always necessary. If you are in a position to take your puppy outside immediately after he eats, that is, snap a leash on him and step out the back door, chances are you can housebreak him at 3 to 5 months of age.

Paper training has its advantages. Even when your dog reaches adulthood, you don't need to take him out for a walk on a rainy or snowy night. You can simply put down some paper, point to it, say, "Do your duties" and the dog will oblige. Same when you go traveling and stop at a hotel or elsewhere. You can use paper and be sure of the dog responding.

As we explained earlier, to paper train your puppy, merely spread out several sheets of newspapers 2 or 3 pages thick in a special corner or area.

Teach your puppy to go on paper.

Spray a little of the "housebreak trainer" on the paper and whenever the puppy begins his sniffing-turning routine just prior to relieving himself, pick him up and put him on the paper. The odor of the trainer will attract him and in a short while he will have learned to use the paper for his duties.

Once again, the key times that a puppy must relieve himself are first thing in the morning when he comes out of his crate, after each meal and after waking up from a sleep. These are the moments you want to be handy and ready to put him on the paper or hurry outside with him.

If you cannot be present because of work or some other reason, put the puppy in a play pen covered with paper (described earlier) or in a room, the entire floor of which should be covered with paper. Using a daily spray of housebreak trainer in the same spot, the puppy quickly learns to go to that special area and the rest of the paper can be removed.

As a puppy grows, his instinct for cleanliness increases. This makes his training easier. Still, he will make some mistakes. Don't lose your temper or patience, just clean it up thoroughly and eliminate all traces and odors so he won't go there again. If you lose your temper, you will only frighten the dog and confuse him so he will tend to hold himself in when you are near, which only sets back his training.

After you have him going pretty well on paper, you can start taking him for walks outside right after meals. Normally he will have to go at this time, and getting him used to the habit will make him enjoy it and begin to hold back after each meal until you can take him out.

In this respect, regularity and routine are important. The more you can practice going out at the same time each day, the easier it will be to train him.

Try to walk him in a place where other dogs have been. The smell of their trademarks will naturally stimulate him to do his on top of it. If you live in the city, this means curbing your dog. It is a law which you should abide by for the sake of other citizens who live there and don't want their sidewalks marred by dog litters.

By using a combination of paper inside and taking your dog for a walk outside after meals, you should be able to housebreak him with relative ease. Talk to him. Tell him in a special tone of voice "Be a good dog, be a good dog." And when he finally goes, praise him thoroughly with, "Good boy! Good boy!" Use the same tone of voice all the time so he learns exactly what you mean.

Once the dog is fairly well housebroken, begin to vary the procedure. Go to a different place by means of a different door or stairway. If a particular spot becomes too firmly fixed in a dog's mind, he may refuse to go anywhere else. Vary the routine so he goes on grass, dirt, gravel, pavement. City dogs have to be taught to relieve themselves in the country when they are there, and country dogs have to be taught to go in the city when necessary.

Also, some dogs become so dependent upon their owners that they will not go when taken out with anyone else. To avoid this, let a neighbor or responsible child walk him occasionally.

Rather than striking the dog when he makes a mistake inside, slap the floor with a rolled-up newspaper as described earlier. You can also scold the dog by looking him in the eye and saying "Shame! Shame on you!" Rubbing his nose in his mistake is no way of training, only a disgusting fallacy that doesn't work.

The young puppy has little control of his bladder, and often petting or an unexpected motion on your part, even a startling sound, will frighten

You should have a set of yard cleaning tools if you have a run for your puppy.

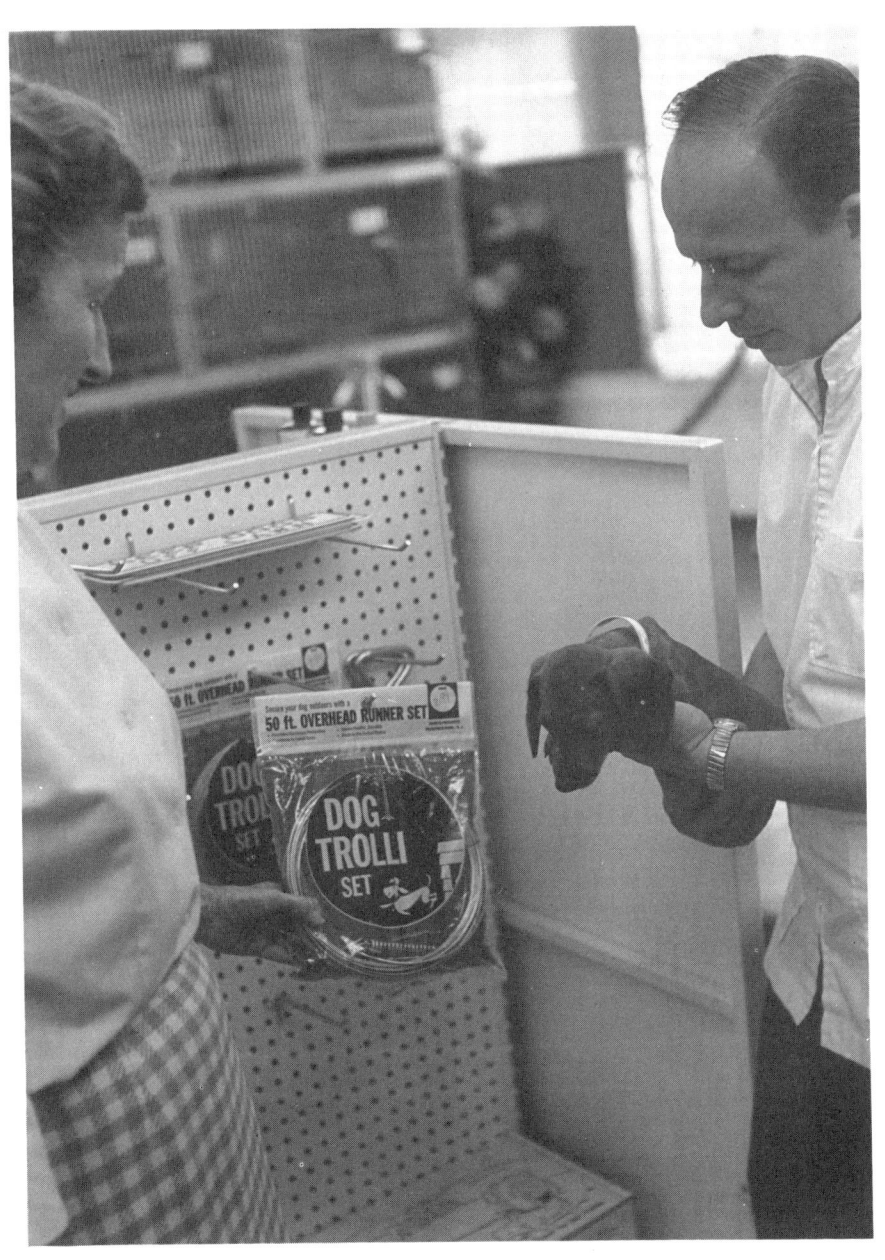

A trolley line can be helpful in exercising and housetraining.

him so he loses control momentarily. He will get over this as he grows up and should never be punished for it.

Remember, too, that cleaning up the mistake thoroughly is a must, otherwise he will most likely be attracted to the spot again. For this, you might buy a can of a special puppy stain remover which removes all traces of odor as well as the spot. We mention this a second time because it is so important, and the cleaning up job so much easier.

Teaching your dog the meaning of shame is valuable when he makes a mistake as an adult as occasionally happens. During illnesses, the beginning of "season," intestinal upsets or visits by a strange dog—these are the times he or she is likely to slip. Whenever your dog is ill, take him out more often or leave paper spread nearby so he can go when he has to.

If a friend or neighbor comes visiting and brings his dog, the perfectly housebroken dog often forgets himself in the excitement. Also, if you have a bitch and your friend's dog is a male, he may begin lifting a leg here and there as a calling card. You shouldn't correct the dog yourself, but feel free to remind your pal in no uncertain terms to mind his dog.

On the very stubborn dog, a special "pet trainer" is effective. After cleaning up the spot where the puppy has voided, bring him to it, show it to him, then spray a bit of the trainer on his front paw, also on the spot. A little of this should be enough.

Also, if your dog or your neighbor's dog relieves himself outside in an area where you don't want him—soiling flower beds, lawn, trees, shrubbery, evergreens—use "dog repellent." It is highly effective in keeping animals away from spots which have been contaminated by urine or feces.

One last hint: if you don't have time to spend with your dog outside, a trolley line or tie-out chain stake will be helpful in his house training. You can snap the puppy on it after each meal, leave him there fifteen minutes and then bring him in. The first time or two it will help if you spray a small area of the ground with a little housebreak trainer. This will help him to understand what is wanted, and once he has started using it, he will go just as soon as you put him on the chain.

Those of you who live in suburbia have the additional concern of cleaning up your dog's feces or droppings in order to get rid of them. For sanitary reasons you cannot leave them on the lawn, and the street cleaners are very infrequent. The best way to clean them up is with one of the metal scoopers designed for the purpose, or you can use a child's toy shovel and hoe. The droppings can either be put in a paper bag and disposed of via the garbage, or can be placed in a can sunken into the ground where they will decompose by themselves or with an occasional sprinkling of an enzymatic digester designed for that purpose.

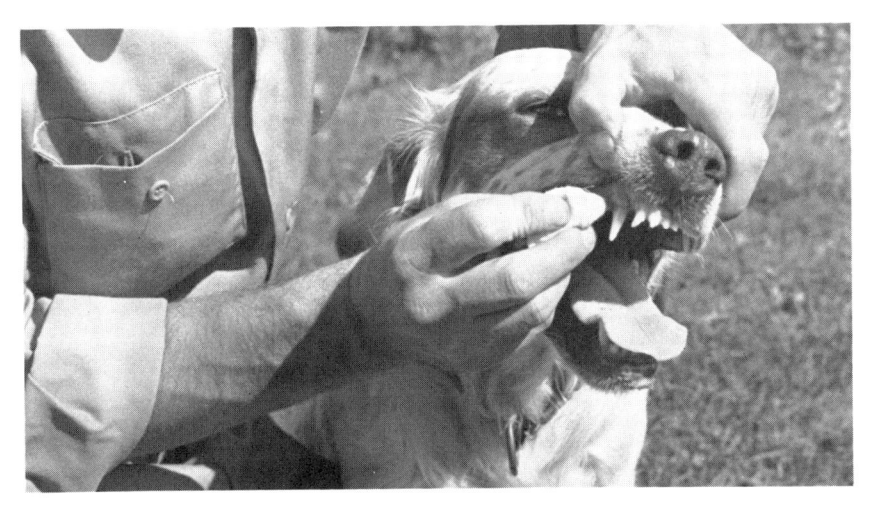

Tartar deposits can do permanent damage to teeth.

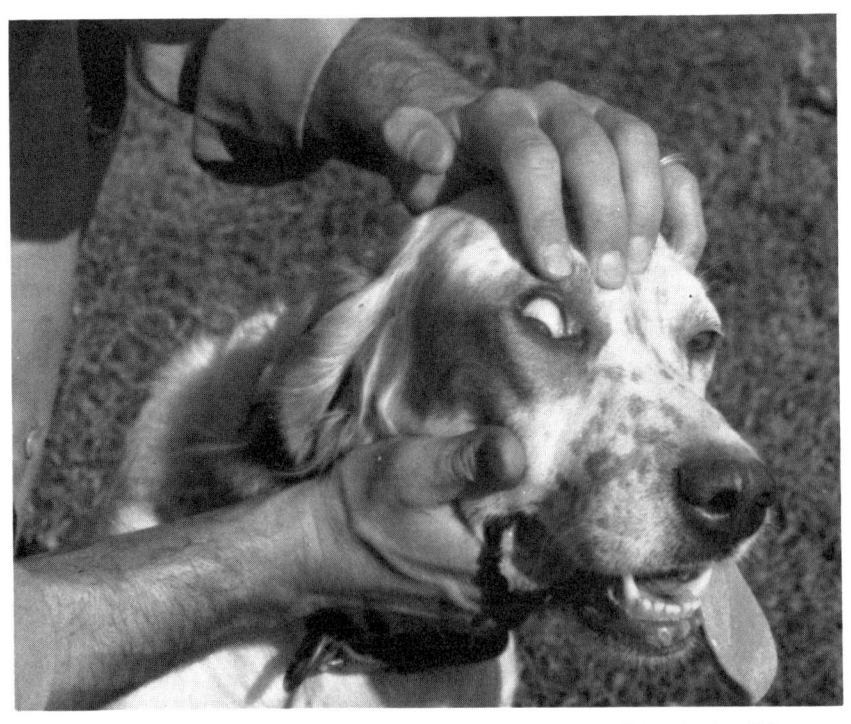

The eye should be bright and clear when you roll back the lid.

4
CARE & GROOMING

Not only should you take pride in your dog but you should take care of him. Since he is completely dependent upon you for everything, the better your care, the better his health will be, also the fewer heartaches and expenses you will have.

Let's start off with the various parts of the dog's body and observe how a little effort on your part will keep him in good condition.

A dog's teeth almost never decay, but they get coated with tartar, especially when the dog is fed soft, mushy food with nothing much to chew on at other times. The tartar deposit is not only an unsightly yellow-grey, but it can do permanent harm to the tooth. When you see it forming, particularly on the rear molars where it always accumulates the heaviest, take your dog to the veterinarian who will scrape them with a dentist's tool.

If your dog likes rawhide bones or "chewies" his mouthing and crunching on them will almost eliminate this condition. They act like a toothbrush, cleaning the teeth, stimulating the gums and the circulation of blood to them. Hard-baked biscuits will do almost as good a job, if your dog likes them. You can also help by wiping his teeth occasionally with a rag and some baking soda. Go over each tooth well and concentrate on the rear ones. Done when the tartar deposits are minor, it will keep them well under control.

Never allow your dog to carry stones around playfully in his mouth. This may look funny in the beginning, and many dogs will do it, but in the process their teeth are worn down, even chipped and broken. Once this happens, they never grow back. Normal retrieving of a ball or canvas boat bumper has no effect on a dog's teeth.

Your dog's eyes are one of his most attractive features. They have been called the "tie that binds him to mankind." In them lies the expression of

Dogs with long ears should have them checked and cleaned often.

entire trust that lifts him above other animals. More than that, by looking at them you can discern a lot about his state of health. The eye should be clear and bright, and when you roll back the lid, the white should not be bloodshot with irritation or washed-out looking. A mucus or pus discharge from the eyes can mean a cold or the beginnings of distemper or other serious infection. The dog's temperature should be taken and if at variance with the 101–102 degree normal, the animal should be inspected immediately by a veterinarian.

In some dogs, particularly toys, the eyes will suffer from excessive weeping which leaves a streak down the cheeks. This can be caused by infection or by over-large tear ducts. There are several eye stain prohibitors available, either through your veterinarian or from any pet shop. Inverted eyelids and in-grown eyelashes can also be the cause of continual weeping and pawing of the eye. In this case it can be cured by minor veterinary surgery.

Your dog's sense of hearing is at least twice as acute as yours, which is how he can hear a so-called "silent" whistle when you can't. It has a frequency higher than is audible to the human ear. Dogs have vastly different kinds of ears. Some stand erect or "pricked"; others are cropped, buttoned or extra long like those of a bloodhound. Sometimes a dog's ears are slow in coming up straight and need to be taped. This is a job for a veterinarian. Make sure you know how your dog's ears should be carried when he is fully grown so early corrections can be made if necessary.

The ear flap, often called the leather, can be a cause of trouble in long-haired dogs. Because the flap covers the inner canal, air has difficulty getting into the ear to dry it, hence you must clean it out once in a while. If you see your dog scratching his ears persistently or shaking his head, you had better check for ear mites. These tiny organisms burrow deep into the ear and can cause deafness if left unattended. Lift the ear flap and examine the inside. If a dark-brown discharge is evident, the ear will have to be cleaned out promptly. The first time you would be wise to have your veterinarian do it so you can watch and see how it is done.

The dog is best placed on his side to work on one ear, then rolled over for the second. Use a cotton ball on the end of your finger to wipe out gently the inside of the ear. Do not use a Q-Tip and probe deeply. Next, the ear can be washed out with a warm solution of half peroxide and half water followed by ear canker powder, or our special ear medicant in liquid form can be used. One or two treatments usually clear up the problem, but your dog's ears should be checked frequently, especially if he has long hair or goes swimming a lot.

His feet also require attention from time to time, the principal thing here being to clip or grind down his nails. In the young puppy, 2 to 6 months of age, this is particularly important because his nails are so sharp that they can ruin nylon stockings and cause "picks" on dresses and furniture material as the puppy romps and plays. A few pinches with a nail clipper will eliminate all this.

The normal activity of your dog after maturity will most likely keep his nails worn down to proper length. If not, they will need clipping or grinding. When the dog stands up straight on his feet, his toenails should not touch the floor. In less active or older dogs, the nails will have to be ground or clipped to keep them in order. Try to avoid hitting the quick which is usually visible if you work in good light. If you happen to touch the quick, use "blood stop" especially designed for stopping the bleeding in this situation.

Giving proper attention to your dog's coat will be an indication of how

Part of puppy grooming is clipping long, sharp toenails.

much pride you take in him. Short-haired dogs naturally need less grooming than medium- and long-haired dogs, but all need to be brushed regularly. The better groomed you keep your dog, the better he will feel and the less hair you will leave around your home or apartment.

    A dog's coat is his complexion. A rich, full, glossy coat means that he is healthy, while a dry lifeless coat with constantly shedding hair indicates a problem. Normally, a dog sheds his coat twice a year, spring and fall, although some shedding goes on all the time. Heavy shedding between seasons may be caused by worms, anemia or the result of illness, while dryness can come from too much bathing or an overheated apartment.

When you groom your dog, either sit on the floor beside him or put him on a table.

If you have a long-haired dog, he should be groomed at least twice a week, preferably every other day. A medium-haired dog does well on one grooming a week. Let your favorite pet shop manager help you with the proper selection of tools for the job. He has a wide selection of combs, brushes, rakes and slicker brushes. He or his assistant can also give you some tips as to how to proceed.

If you neglect to comb out your dog when he is shedding, mats of dead hair will form at various places on his body and be very difficult to get out. In some cases they will have to be cut out, so keep up the combing and brushing. Clogs of tar or chewing gum can be removed by rubbing them with a piece of ice. Tangles of burrs, beggar lice and other weeds can be removed by working them out with your fingers and a little mineral oil.

When you start grooming, either sit on the floor beside your dog or place him on a table so you both will be comfortable. Make your dog stand mannerly while you work on him. As soon as he learns you are out to help him, he'll begin to cooperate. Some breeds have to be brushed, some plucked and some combed. Learn how your dog should be handled. You probably won't be able to do it yourself at first, but probably your pet shop has full grooming facilities and after a few sessions done professionally, you can give it a try yourself if you wish.

Certain breeds such as the Poodle require clipping and special hair styling. These are best done by a professional at first, otherwise the amateur may come off with a rather sorry looking animal. You have a choice of several clips for your Poodle, the most popular being the Royal Dutch, but the breed ring requires that he sport either an English Saddle or Continental clip in order to be eligible for showing. If you want to clip your own Poodle, the best way is to have a professional do it the first few times, then you can start to follow the outline of the pattern. Working the electric clippers and scissors around the face, neck and feet without cutting the dog is a feat not to be attempted the first time. Better have this done in the beginning by someone who knows, then later perhaps you can give it a try yourself.

Occasionally you may want to bathe your dog. It is the proper thing to do once your puppy is five or six months of age. If you do it outside, pick a warm day. Inside, use the basin or bath tub, depending upon the size of the dog, and have the room well heated so he will dry quickly. There are several outstanding shampoos at pet shops you can use. They are milder on the coat than hand soap.

In preparing your dog for his bath, stuff a small ball of cotton in each ear, and put a drop of mineral oil in each eye to keep water and soap out of them. Stand him in comfortably warm water up to the middle of his legs, leaving yourself enough room to hand-scrub him underneath. Wet him thoroughly all over by ladling the water over his back, neck and shoulders with a cup or pan. Talk to him so he isn't frightened. Apply the shampoo and work it into a lather, shaping him from the top of the head to the tip of his tail. Don't skip anything. Work around the root of his tail, underbody, legs and feet. Rinse quickly, then soap again. The first soaping loosens the dirt and the second removes it. Give him a thorough rinsing, being sure to wash out all the soap. A slight amount left in the hair to dry causes dandruff and scratching.

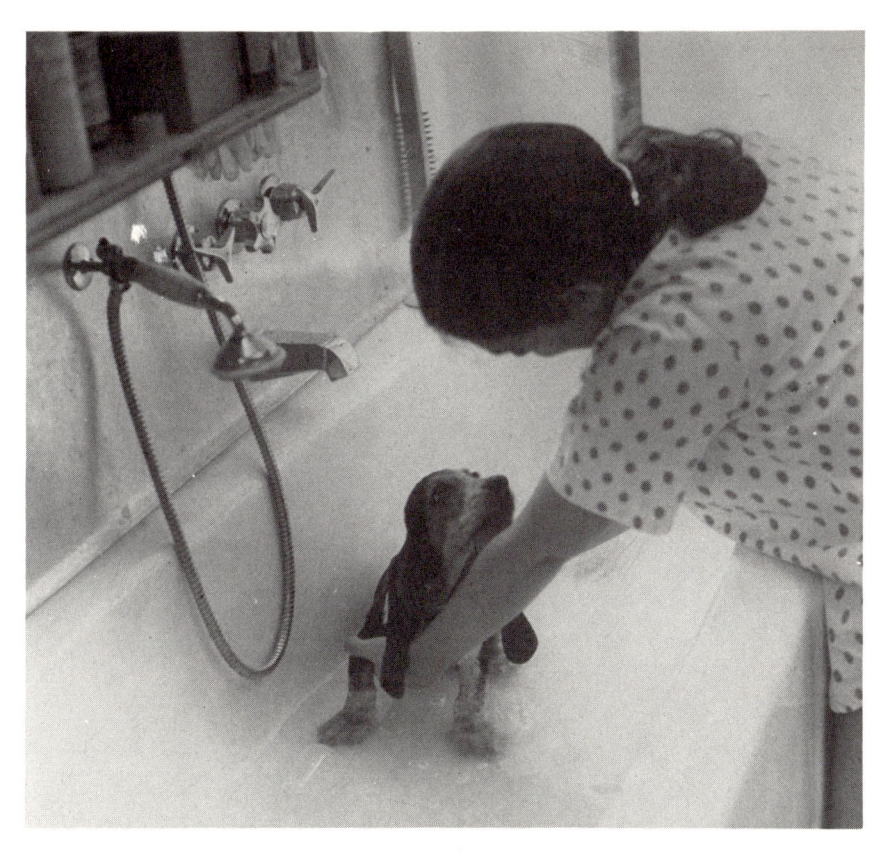

When washing your puppy, stand him in comfortably warm water up to his knees.

When finished, lift the dog from the tub and dry him with Turkish towels. If he has a heavy coat, go slowly and take plenty of time. You can use a hot-air electric dryer if you think it will help. Keep the dog out of drafts until completely dry, which can take up to two hours in the case of a heavy coat. Don't brush or comb the coat while the dog is still wet. You'll pull out too much of the coat.

You can give your dog a bath every two to three months if you wish. Try to get him to enjoy it. Talk to him so he cooperates. The occasional dog that fights it all the way will require help from another member of the family. A dog should not fear his bath, and it is the first few times of initiation that count.

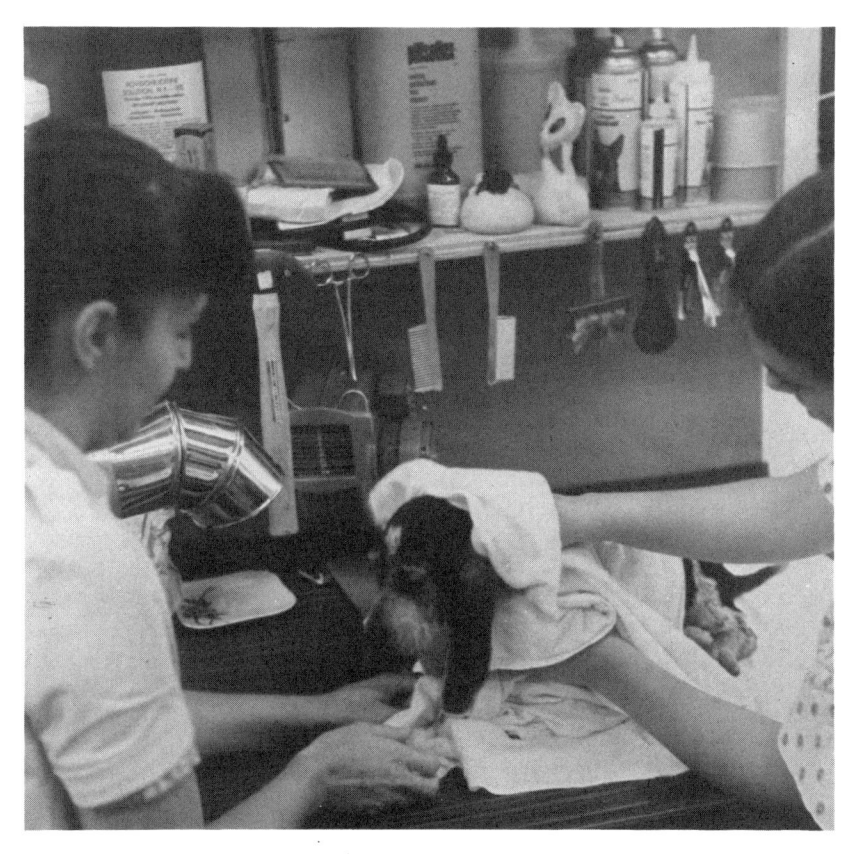

Dry him with a bath towel and hair dryer.

If for some reason you cannot or don't want to give your dog a wet bath, it is possible to give him a "dry cleaning." There are special cleansing agents in both liquid and dry form which can be worked into the dog's coat, then wiped off with a towel. Although not as effective as washing, they serve well in cold weather or when you want to cut down on doggy odors and haven't time to wash him.

5
HOUSING

MOTTO FOR A DOG HOUSE
I love this little house because
It offers, after dark,
A pause for rest, a rest for paws,
A place to moor my bark.
—*Arthur Guiterman*

The ways that you can house your dog are as varied as the situation in which you live. Not everyone keeps his dog in an apartment or home, and even if he does, there are several methods of doing it.

The apartment dog, as we said in the beginning, is best housed in a wire or wooden crate at night. This becomes his home, his corner of security, and it forms the basis for the easiest method to housebreak him. When you have to leave him alone for a few hours, you can confine him to his crate or to any small room. When you go on a trip, the wire folding crate goes along and becomes his home away from home. In later years, he can be given the privilege of sleeping on your bed at night if you wish, but while still a puppy, this can cause problems in training and discipline.

Some people keep the dog in the cellar of their home, especially if he is an extra large one. This is all right providing it is not a dark, damp, poorly ventilated place. Assuming that the area is light, dry and airy, it can serve as his bedroom at night, but not as a constant place of living. A wood platform should be constructed for the dog a few inches off the floor, with sides for protection against drafts. A foam or cotton mattress that is at the same time a repellent against fleas can be added for his comfort. We do not recommend keeping your dog in the cellar unless it is absolutely necessary.

You would do better to keep your dog outside, and there is no reason why you should not if he is a sturdy specimen of the sporting or working breeds. For this you will need a well-made, year-round house and a fenced-in run. Many dog owners keep their pet outside much of the time for watchdog or hunting purposes and bring him into the house in the afternoon or even for a few hours of companionship and enjoyment each day.

The year-round dog house (see photo, next page) should be constructed of $\frac{1}{2}''$ plywood, exterior type, with a pitched roof that is hinged so it can be lifted for airing in the summer and easy cleaning. The baffle panel inside provides draft-free comfort for the dog in temperatures as low as zero degrees F. The dog's body heat will keep him warm, especially when a good bedding of cedar shavings, straw or hay is added.

Some puppies love a wicker basket to sleep in.

The year-round outdoor house should have a divider for winter and be on stilts so the dog can crawl under for shade in the summer.

The house should be built on stilts about a foot high so the dog can crawl underneath in the summer and stay cool. Also, if he is at all active, he will jump up on the roof several times a day to look around, and this makes for excellent exercise. The house should face the south or east for protection against storms and weather. The Air Corps guard dogs have individual houses on posts that swing with the wind, always facing in the opposite direction, but this feature is hardly necessary.

A dog who has his own house outdoors should have a fenced-in run rather than be chained or placed on a trolley. A dog with any size to him will pull down a trolley within a week, and constant chaining is inclined to make a dog vicious or mean in temperament. Children and other dogs tease him by going near but not quite close enough for him to reach them.

A run you can build yourself is made out of heavy-duty wire and wooden posts but the best kind is chain link paneling which can be moved or rearranged at any time on your property. Or, if you move to another home, the fence can be taken down and carried right along with you. These panels are pipe framing to which chain link wire is tightly stretched. They come in various lengths and heights, with sturdy gates to match. The small dog requires a four-foot fence; the medium-sized dog a five-foot fence; the large dog a six-foot fence. A top can be included if desired, but chain link is next to impossible for a dog to scale.

Anchor fencing is the toughest and most permanent of all. For this, posts are sunk into the ground in concrete, and chain link wire attached to this. It is not only expensive, but once put up, it cannot be moved. The panel run will cost about the same but has the advantage of being portable.

In designing a dog run, you should make it long and narrow rather than square. A dog will gain considerable exercise running up and down a run that has length, whereas he will fail to utilize the space in a square arrangement. The run should be four to six feet wide and ten to fifty feet long, depending upon your yard size and pocketbook. The gate is usually at one end.

The base of the run can be dirt, asphalt, gravel or concrete. Dirt is the least desirable from not only a health standpoint but digging out as well. It usually lacks good drainage and tends to harbor worm eggs, urine smells, even unhealthy viruses. An asphalt run is easy to install but it is rather hot in the summer unless ample shade is provided. A concrete run is most easy to maintain and keep sanitary; it should be pitched for drainage and have a tree nearby for shade in the summer because it too gets hot in the sun. This is the type used by most kennels and veterinary

This post-and-rail fence with wire inside gives your dog some freedom and allows him to protect the house also.

establishments; it usually includes gutters which drain into a sump or cesspool. A gravel run is best of all for a dog's feet but is more difficult to clean and keep raked. All runs should be sprayed at least once a week during the summer for disinfection and odor control.

Some people compromise by keeping their dog in the home and fencing in their back yard for him to use as a giant run. This has the advantage of spaciousness for romp and play and is ideal for toys and other small dogs. But large dogs require high fences and their eliminations tend to become bothersome and unsightly unless they can be trained to use one area. A post and rail fence, lined with 12½-gauge 2×4″ mesh wire, makes a most attractive area for a small dog and allows him plenty of room for exercise as well as protective activities for the home.

If you have an outdoor run or fenced-in back yard for your dog, though he lives mainly in the house, you may want a special shelter house for him. It is ideal protection for sunny and rainy days and is rust-proof.

The very best arrangement for your dog to act as guardian of the home is to keep him inside and have a come-go door which he can push through to go out or enter at will. As shown in the sketch, his run begins at the front corner of the house and follows along one side to the back door. This allows him to watch all activity at both the front and back doors, which he soon learns to do if he is at all protective by nature. Also, this set-up eliminates the need to walk the dog. He is easily taught simply to go outside and relieve himself in his run whenever he is so inclined.

His run, which follows along the side of the house, should be made of

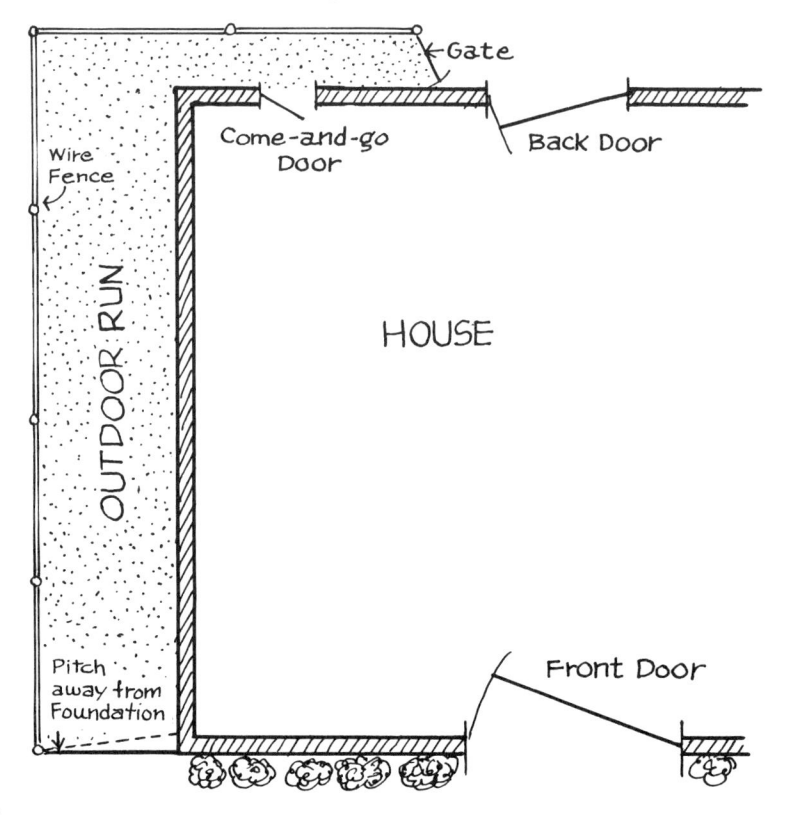

When planning a run, make it long and narrow. Panel fencing shown here is easily movable.

poured concrete pitched away from the foundation. Because one side of the house is utilized, only half the amount of fencing is needed which cuts costs considerably. A gate should be located near the back of the run. The fencing should be five or six feet high and may be screened by attractive shrubbery. For those who want thorough watchdog protection for their home, this is the ideal arrangement and is being used by many people in suburbia today.

6

KEEPING YOUR PUPPY HEALTHY

The health of your puppy depends mainly upon the day-to-day care you give it. Good food, adequate sleeping quarters, regular grooming, all play their roles. Exercise is important, particularly if he is of an active breed. He shouldn't be turned loose to run free on his own; this is one of the worst things you can do as we will explain shortly. But a daily walk or run with the master is necessary for general good health. Swimming is another excellent form of exercise. Most dogs love water if properly introduced to it.

How do you tell if your dog is healthy?

There are several telltale signs if he is not. An unpleasant, mopish hunchbacked look can mean something internally wrong. A poor coat that is dry and lacks bloom, dull eyes, gums and inside of lips a dull cream or white indicate anemia from worms, as do loose stools streaked with blood. Hard, chalky stools are a sign of constipation. Abnormal consumption of water points to kidney trouble or fever. Loss of skin elasticity means serious dehydration. Although all of these may be meaningless to you when you see them in your dog, it means he needs help promptly.

External parasites—fleas, ticks, flies and mange mites—cause as much damage to a dog's skin and general well being as anything else. It used to be thought that fleas were the greatest dog exercisers in the world, but now that we know all the skin disease they cause, we realize the fallacy of this. There is no excuse for having fleas or ticks on your dog any more. You can buy a flea collar that is very effective in ridding your dog of

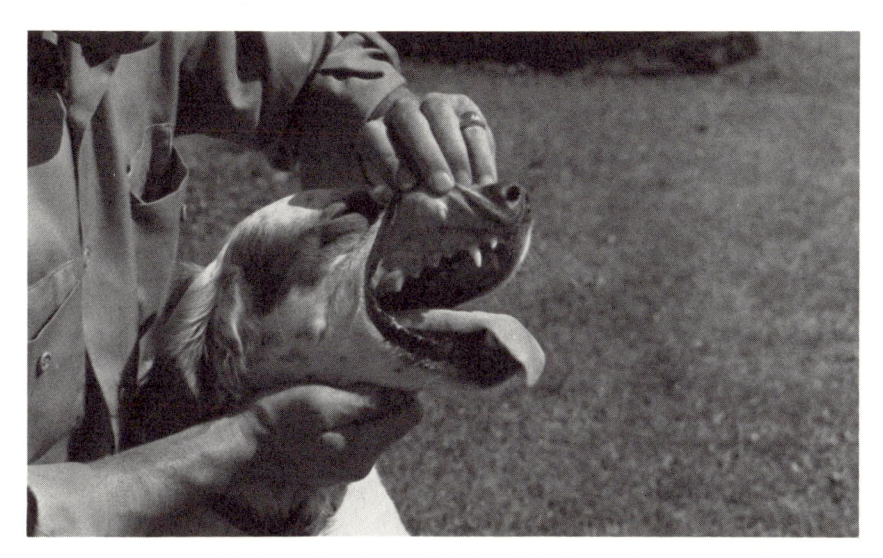

A healthy dog has a bright pink lip and gums.

The skin on your dog's back should jump back into place if he is healthy.

them. He simply wears it along with his regular collar, and it has a three-month effectiveness during the summer months when fleas are most prevalent. Or you can use a special flea and tick spray in an aerosol can. It kills fleas, ticks and lice, repels annoying flies, gnats and mosquitoes, checks scratching and contains lanolin for conditioning the coat.

You should keep your dog free from fleas and ticks just to make sure they never get in your house or apartment. These pests lodge in furniture bindings, picture frame moldings and other cracks where they breed in overwhelming numbers. Professional exterminators are then needed to bring them under control.

While on the subject, there are other kinds of canine skin problems you should know about. Wet eczema (also called "summer hot spots") comes generally from the dog scratching or licking a certain spot until it is hairless, red and weeping fluid. There is also dry eczema which dulls the coat and creates dandruff as a result of dietary or metabolic imbalances. Mange is an insidious skin disease that attacks the roots of the hair and puts the dog in a most unsightly, sore-covered condition. The sarcoptic type is highly contagious among dogs but easier to cure than the demotectic type. When out walking with your pet, be sure to keep him away from any dog which has patches of hair missing. And if any hairless spots appear on your dog's skin, take him to your veterinarian for treatment at once. Prompt attention will keep it from spreading over his body.

Another kind of parasite that affects dogs severely is worms. There are five kinds—roundworms, tapeworms, hookworms, whipworms and heartworms. All except heartworms are located in the intestinal tract where they live on the dog's blood and nutritional intake, draining much of his vital strength from him. Heartworms are located in the heart itself and are a very serious condition which, if left unchecked, can kill a dog.

Roundworms are often visible in the dog's stool and resemble pieces of spaghetti about an inch or two long. They are the most common and easiest of all worms to get rid of. Puppies are often born with them. Be sure your pet has been carefully wormed before you take him home.

Tapeworms can be seen in the stool as flesh-colored, square-shaped segments not unlike pieces of noodles. In the air, they dry brownish and often remain attached to the dog's rectum like dried grains of rice. This parasite can be several feet long and continue to grow unless the head is eliminated. Strong medicine is required to fully remove tapeworms and should be administered by a veterinarian.

Hookworms attach themselves to the intestinal walls of the dog and suck his blood. They are too small to be visible to the naked eye but are readily seen under a microscope as are the eggs. Hookworms seriously

Control fleas and ticks on your dog with flea powder.

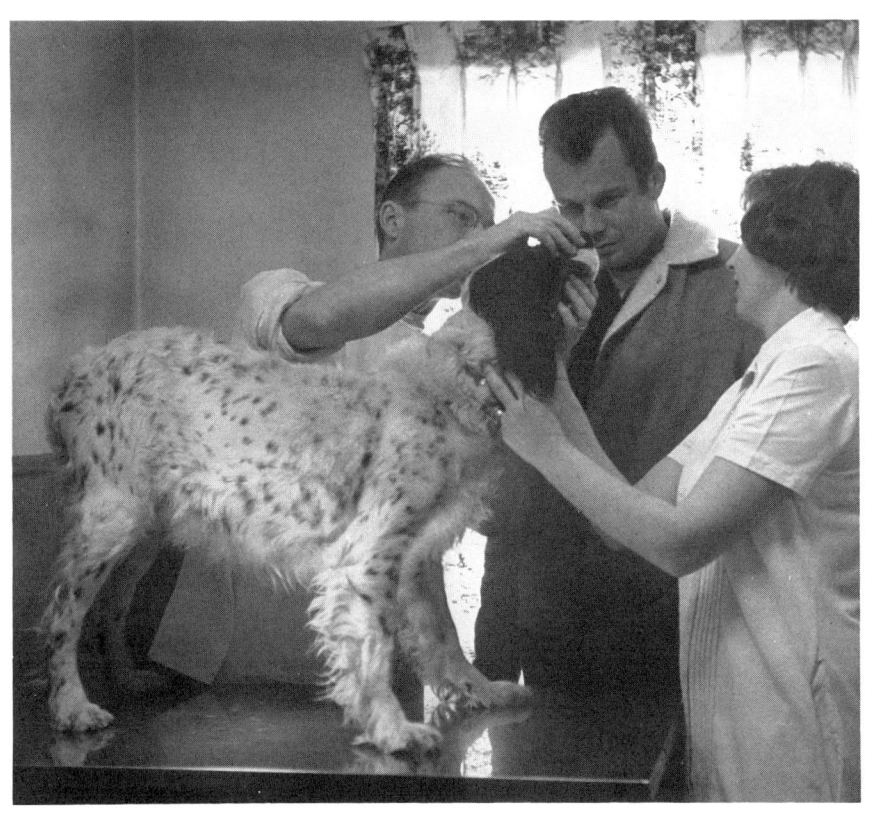

Establish a close relationship with your veterinarian.

drain a dog's strength but can now be controlled more easily than just a few years ago. Several methods are possible, depending upon the severity of the case.

Whipworms are about two inches long but seldom seen in the stool because they live mainly in the cecum (a pocket similar to the human appendix) and thus are difficult to treat. For a long time the best approach was an injection into the bloodstream or an operation for removal of the cecum. Now there are new insecticides which can do the job more easily.

Heartworms were once restricted to the mosquito country of the South, because the disease is transported primarily by that insect, but in recent years it has spread to almost all parts of the country because of carrier dogs. Tiny organisms called microfilaria, live in the bloodstream and attach themselves to the ventricals of the heart where they mature into fine, wire-like worms one to four inches long, gradually slowing down the action of the heart and finally overwhelming it. Diagnosis and treatment must be done by a veterinarian.

Most dogs have worms at one time or another, some more seriously than others. When allowed to go unchecked and multiply, they can severely debilitate your pet to the point where his resistance is so lowered that he cannot throw off other diseases. Symptoms are about the same in all cases of intestinal worms: pale gums and eyes, loss of weight, dull coat, diarrhea, anemia. Sometimes a dog heavily infested with tapeworms will scoot along the ground or carpet on his rectum, indicating itching, though this can also mean that the anal glands need attention.

There are some excellent worm treatments available today. The thing to do is have your dog's stool checked twice a year by your veterinarian, a very simple and inexpensive process. Put a sizeable portion of a fresh stool in a plastic bag and deliver it to his laboratory.

A heartworm check is more complicated and requires a blood sample which must then be analyzed. Ask your veterinarian if the incidence of heartworm in your area is high enough to warrant an examination. Symptoms in your dog are lack of stamina, quick exhaustion, difficult breathing, perhaps even collapse in advanced cases.

Earlier we spoke about the importance of vaccinating your dog against distemper, hepatitis and leptospirosis—the three great enemies of the dog world. Again we remind you that not only is it necessary to have one shot, but a series. If you do not and your dog is stricken by one of these virulent diseases, you will forever regret your mistake. Though distemper attacks the nervous system, hepatitis the liver, and leptospirosis the kidneys, the symptoms are all quite similar. The dog's nose becomes dry and encrusted, eyes inflamed and sensitive to light. Lung congestion causes coughing, air-hunger extends the neck in open-mouthed gasping, finally convulsions.

More serious and discouraging is the way in which distemper often shatters the nervous system, immobilizing the hindquarters and causing derangement, whining, restlessness. Even if you succeed in nursing the dog to recovery by forced hand feeding, he may be permanently affected by a twitch or blindness.

As a rule, hepatitis starts off with a very high temperature (104 to 106 degrees), then drops. The dog develops a humped appearance and is very sore to the touch in the abdominal region. There is a rapid loss of weight and appetite, vomiting of a yellowish liquid, and a tarry stool. Rapid death occurs in many cases, but if the dog survives, he is usually well on the way to recovery in two to seven days and immune to the disease the rest of his life.

Weigh the big dog on bathroom scales.

DHL, as they are called, are more likely to strike the younger dogs than older ones, the city and suburban dogs rather than country ones because the former are more exposed. The virus of each disease remains viable longer in cold weather than in warmth and sunshine, making the possibility of infection greater in winter than in summer. Initial resistance to DHL is determined by the puppy's natural immunity passed on by its mother at birth. Viruses of DHL are spread directly (one dog touching another through a fence or on a leash) or indirectly (through the feces and urine). Dogs that recover from hepatitis or leptospirosis can be carriers for long periods while showing no signs of infection. This is why an annual booster shot is strongly recommended, so that the level of immunity can be kept high.

You will find it handy to know a few things about treating your dog—taking his temperature, weighing, etc.

Buy a thermometer and use it. The hot-nose test to tell a dog's temperature isn't reliable. Petroleum jelly should be applied as a lubricant to the thermometer which is then inserted rectally. Have the dog on his side for better control. If you hold his head down and talk soothingly to him, he'll stop squirming and lie still. The thermometer must remain half way inserted in the anus at least two minutes. The temperature should be between 101 and 102 degrees; much above or below these figures indicates trouble.

You will need to weigh your dog at times, either for the administering of medicine by the pound or to check if he is losing or gaining weight properly. Puppies and toy dogs that are not jumpy can be weighed on kitchen scales. Larger dogs must be picked up in your arms while you step on a pair of bathroom scales, then afterwards weigh yourself and subtract the difference to determine the poundage of the dog.

To administer a pill to your dog, put him in a sitting position (if he tries to squirm away, squeeze him tightly between your legs as you squat behind him). Hold his mouth open with your left hand, his head slightly elevated. With the pill held between the thumb and index finger of the right hand, dip it in some water or oil so it will slide easily, then push the pill as far to the back of the dog's mouth and down his throat as possible. Withdraw your hand quickly, close his mouth with both hands and hold his muzzle up firmly at a forty-five degree angle until he swallows.

Liquid medication is simple to give. With your dog in a sitting position, muzzle raised upwards, pour the liquid from the spoon or bottle inside the dog's cheek. It will run into his mouth and down his throat.

7
FIRST AID

Often there comes a time when your dog will meet with some mishap requiring first aid. The success of the emergency depends upon speed. The longer you wait, the more critical the condition becomes, consequently the less time a veterinarian has to diagnose and cope with the situation.

The simplest cure for every accident is to prevent it from happening. For example, when a dog is turned loose and allowed to wander, he runs the highest risk of mishap that he can possibly face. He is constantly subject to auto accidents, theft, poisoning, dog fights, glass cuts and all sorts of calamity beyond imagination. The person who allows his dog to run at large is really abusing him and should be denied the right of owning one. Not only does such a dog become a nuisance to the neighbors but it will inevitably bring about its own downfall.

Other preventive measures include eliminating sharp, protruding objects in the dog's living area, either in the home or kennel. Rusty nails and hooks can cause serious injury. Keep the lids locked on garbage cans, and avoid placing rat poison as well as other toxins, roach powders or garden sprays where he can smell them or walk through them.

Discipline is a prime method of accident prevention. A puppy may pull on a lamp cord or jump against a flower stand, and the falling objects cause him serious injury. Teach your dog manners just as you would a child.

In approaching any dog after an accident, speak to him over and over. Chances are that his first reaction will be to defend himself and unless he recognizes that you represent help, he may try to bite. After you have gained his attention, reassure him with kind words and move in cautiously. Take a piece of gauze or a necktie or stocking, loop it over the bridge of his nose and knot it under his chin locking his jaws together, then bring the loose ends around each side of his neck and knot them securely

Administer a pill this way.

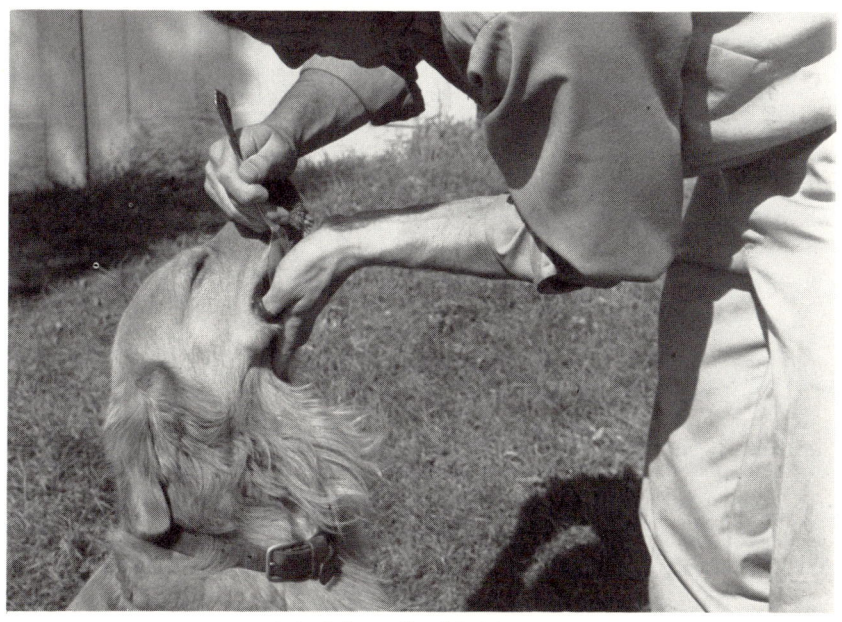

Administer liquid this way.

Make a gauze muzzle for your dog if he is injured.

behind his ears. This simple muzzle will provide protection for you while working on the dog. If you can't find a rope, put a heavy coat over his head, pinning his head down so he can still breathe but not bite.

It is always best to have assistance, particularly when moving a dog. Improvise a stretcher by using a blanket, coat, plywood board, etc., and proceed gently, especially if he has been hit by a car or is unconscious from shock or bloat.

In the case of burns, where they are mild, trim away the hair and apply an aerosol spray remedy used for humans or an ointment of tannic acid base. Lacking these, use strong tea, applied through a gauze bandage taped lightly over the burned area. A bicarbonate-of-soda solution may also be used.

Clipper burns which come from careless grooming can be treated with an aerosol spray for burns. Never apply strong antiseptics such as iodine to a burn for it will only aggravate the condition.

In cases of severe burns or scalds, get the dog to a veterinary hospital as quickly as possible. He will be in extreme pain, so handle him with considerable caution. If he falls into shock, keep him warm with a hot water bottle or electric pad.

Never attempt to give an unconscious animal stimulants. You may choke him to death. Try reviving him with a whiff of smelling salts or ammonia. If he is conscious, a little whiskey half strength or some good black coffee will help his state of shock. Pour it slowly between his side teeth and cheek with his head raised.

A dog's feet can be very painfully burned when he runs over hot tar from a newly surfaced road or driveway. Your first impulse is to pour a solvent such as gasoline or cleaning fluid over the dog's pads, but this is the worst possible thing you could do as it aggravates the burn intensely. Instead, work cold cream or some lanolin-base oil gently into the pads until the tar is loosened.

Sprains often occur in little dogs around the home. They jump boldly off a chair or bed and damage the ligaments of their legs, causing severe lameness though no visible signs of injury appear. The dog must be kept as quiet as possible and ice packs applied to reduce the swelling. The soreness can be helped by liniment.

Fractures often occur in the small bones of a dog's foot as a result of falling, being stepped on, etc. A veterinarian will have to X-ray the foot and set it in a cast or splint.

If your dog severely fractures a leg, place it in a temporary splint to prevent further damage. A front leg should be padded with a soft cloth, then wrapped in several thicknesses of newspaper to form a tube. If a

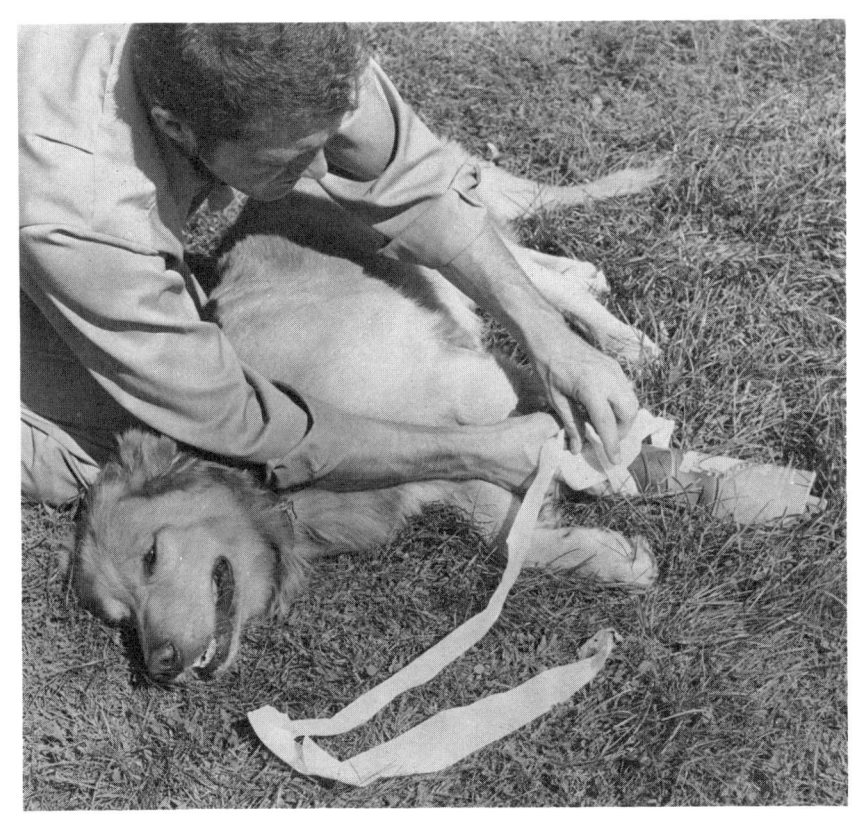

An emergency leg splint can be made of rolled-up magazine or board.

hind leg, you can tape it to a smooth flat board for support but not tight enough to impair circulation. Veterinary work on fractures is little short of miraculous these days, but one of the secrets is immediate treatment.

Often a puppy, occasionally an old dog, will swallow a foreign object which can cause severe internal damage if not fatality unless it is removed. Toys, needles, fishhooks, bone splinters are commonly removed by surgery from dogs' stomachs, intestines and esophagus. It must be done before peritonitis sets in.

If you are positive your dog has swallowed something, call your veterinarian and ask if it can be safely passed. If you are in a position where you must treat the dog yourself, feed it (force-feed it if necessary) some soft food like bread and milk, then follow quickly with an emetic which will cause the dog to vomit. If you are fortunate, the foreign object will come up with the soft food. For an emetic, use either two teaspoons of salt in a cup of warm water or the old reliable teaspoon of mustard, both of which must be forced down the dog's throat.

Dogs will cut and scratch themselves from time to time as they run through briars or step on glass. Usually their own licking, which is very curative, will take care of the situation. If the scratch warrants attention, it should be washed with soap and water and an antiseptic applied. You may want to clip the hair from the area first, otherwise the dog may chew it away if he has a long coat. Bandaging a minor cut is hardly worth the effort. The dog will remove it the moment you turn your back.

If the cut is serious enough to require stitches, let your veterinarian do the suturing and apply a bandage which can be sprayed with a bitter tasting repellent to keep the dog from chewing it.

One of the by-products of modern living is the widespread use of poisons in a variety of forms for the control of undesirable animal and insect life. Unfortunately this often leads to the contamination of desirable animals such as pets. Your dog can be floored by walking through certain chemical fertilizers and licking his pads or sniffing roach powder or chewing the lead-base paint on his dog house or gobbling up some old pills or toxic food while nosing through a garbage pail. DDT will cause poisoning, as will a wobbly rat, half dead from thallium. Other odd poisons are typical to certain parts of the country. Blowfish, discarded by fishermen along the Florida and Gulf coastlines, can be deadly, as well as certain types of mushrooms in northerly regions.

When you see your pet stagger blindly into a wall or begin writhing and groaning in agony, if he looks aimless or near a state of collapse, vomiting or in convulsions, the cause may be poison, so act quickly.

Check around and see if you can find the container which was the cause. It will list the proper antidote. There are many poisons. Treatment for each is different, which makes it vitally important to find what type the dog consumed. Call your veterinarian and take the dog and container to him immediately.

If you are forced to treat the dog yourself and don't know the specific poison, it is best to induce vomiting. As an emetic, use a teaspoon of mustard in a cup of warm water, or two teaspoons of salt in a cup of warm water, or hydrogen peroxide mixed half and half with water. This can be followed by milk and egg white, then equal parts of milk of magnesia and mineral oil. In some cases artificial respiration is necessary, and the temperature of the dog should be watched carefully so that collapse can be avoided.

If your dog is involved in an auto accident, be careful about moving him, especially if he is severely injured. Use the emergency muzzle for your protection and handle the dog with great care. If any bones appear broken, keep them as straight as possible. Move the dog on a hard, flat surface like a board rather than on a saggy blanket, and keep his head slightly above the rest of his body for better breathing.

Bad cuts can be bandaged temporarily with a cloth or handkerchief to check bleeding. Tie them loosely so as not to impair circulation. The head or any part of the body can be bandaged if necessary.

Profuse bleeding from a cut means an artery has been severed, in which case you'll have to apply a tourniquet to stop it. The tourniquet can be a piece of rope or cloth. It must be placed between the cut and the heart and twisted tight enough to stop the bleeding. Loosen it every fifteen minutes for a few moments so that circulation can resume, thus avoiding gangrene, then retighten it. The dog will probably suffer from shock and should be kept warm by means of a blanket. Get him to a veterinarian as soon as possible.

Dog fights are nasty things in which the two animals fight till one gives up and runs or sometimes dies. Separating them can be difficult and usually requires the full strength of two brave people. Beating or whipping only incites them more, and if you try to pull them apart, you most likely will get bitten in the process. Squirting water on them with a garden hose sometimes works, as does a bucket of water. The most effective way is to use an electric shock stick or cattle prod. This never fails.

If you have a dog which shows a tendency to fight, train him out of it right in the beginning. Buy an electric shock stick and any time he starts for a dog while on a lead, pop him on the shoulder with it. He'll change his attitude in a hurry. If you don't want to teach him yourself, take him to a professional trainer.

If your dog is chewed up in a fight, his skin will be full of puncture wounds, perhaps a ripped ear or jagged skin lesion that will need suturing. The cuts must be cleaned out, and an antibiotic injection should be given by your veterinarian.

Dogs love to tangle with skunks, although nothing is more annoying. Many leading pet shops sell a good deodorant; lacking this, you can saturate the dog with tomato juice. Leave it on overnight and wash the dog the next day. If he digs at his eyes after a skunk encounter, some of the spray has gotten into them. For relief, wash them out with boric acid solution or a good eye medication.

One of the most painful and pitiful things that can happen to your

It is possible to give a dog artificial respiration.

dog is to become involved with a porcupine. His face and head will look like a pin cushion from the barbed quills. They must be removed as quickly as possible, otherwise they will work deeper into the flesh. Try to get the dog to a veterinarian because it's such a painful job that an anesthetic should be given. If you do it yourself, give the dog a sedative from a country drug store or at least a couple of aspirins. Use a small

73

If you live in a poison snake area, it is worthwhile having a snakebite kit.

pair of pincer pliers and work slowly, with a steady pull on each one. Don't try to jerk them out. Afterwards, clean each wound with peroxide or any other antiseptic.

Bee stings are not unusual, particularly among shorthaired dogs. On the body they cause little difficulty, but around the eyes, ears and underside of the dog they can be painful and cause swelling. Daub the spot with a paste made of bicarbonate of soda and water. If you are out in the woods, some good cold mud will help. If the dog happens to be stung profusely, a veterinarian should treat him, for he will need both a local anesthetic and a counteractant for the poison. Bee stings to an allergic dog can be fatal.

Quite frequently farm and hunting dogs, even suburban dogs come upon snakes unexpectedly and are bitten, or tease them until it happens.

Bites of rattlesnakes, copperheads, moccasins and coral snakes can easily mean death unless you know what to do.

Snake bites require immediate treatment. The majority of fatalities result from waiting too long. To avoid this, one should have on hand a snake bite kit and have carefully studied the directions in advance so you know how to mix and prepare the serum, how to manage the large and small vial which, when placed together, become a syringe and when reversed, make a suction cup. The time you waste reading and applying these instructions after your dog has been bitten, could mean the difference between his life and death.

Snakes usually strike the nose or legs of a dog. The bite can be found by two tiny punctures in the skin where the fangs entered. In a matter of moments painful swelling develops, followed most likely by vomiting, convulsions, difficult breathing, finally collapse and death.

After the punctures are located, it is best to muzzle the dog because two small deep incisions with a razor blade must be made in the form of an "X" over each puncture. If the bite is on a leg, apply a tourniquet tightly between it and the heart. After the incisions have been made, as much blood as possible should be drawn from the wound, either by the suction cup, squeezing, or by sucking on it with your mouth and spitting out the tainted blood (be sure you have no cuts in your mouth). Wash the

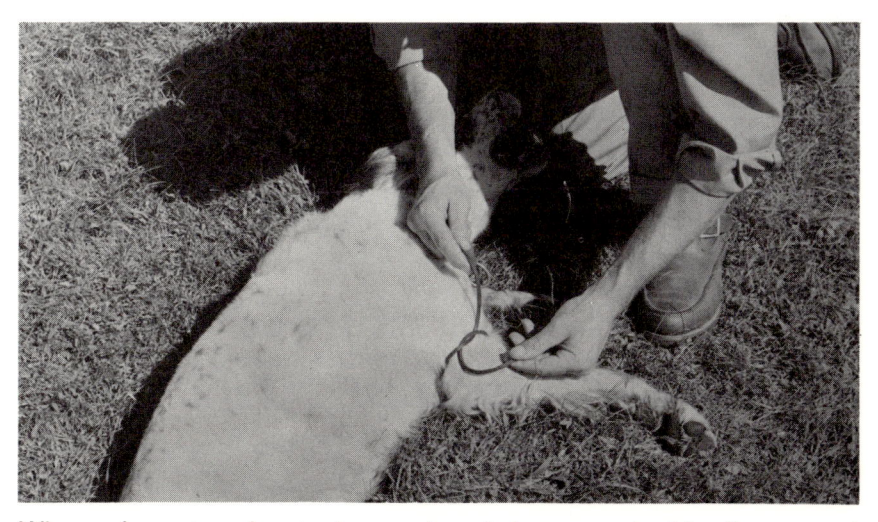

When using a tourniquet, always place it between the bleeding wound and heart. Cloth, belt, rope or shoelace will do.

75

Start your own first aid kit for emergencies.

wound, then use the serum. Release the tourniquet every twenty minutes for a brief period to prevent gangrene.

If your dog is bitten by a snake, try to keep him as inactive as possible. Don't lead him out of the woods to the car, carry him; the more activity, the faster the poison will circulate. If you treat him in the woods, keep him warm and quiet; also when driving him to a veterinarian. Above all, know what to do, and do it quickly.

As we mentioned earlier and as you can now appreciate, it is wise to put together a first aid kit that can be kept handy for all emergencies. Speak to your veterinarian about it. He can make valuable suggestions and additions that may require prescriptions. Basically it should include the following:

1. Cotton roll and swabs
2. Adhesive tape roll one inch wide
3. Roll of gauze
4. A wound powder or aerosol spray (see your veterinarian)
5. An antiseptic (hydrogen peroxide or scarlet oil which is a great healer but stains the dog and surroundings)
6. A prepared emetic for poisoning (see your veterinarian)
7. An eye wash and an eye medicant
8. Stout pair of tweezers
9. Antibiotic (see your veterinarian)
10. Petroleum jelly
11. Thermometer
12. Snake Bite Kit and package of sealed razor blades
13. Tourniquet
14. Muzzle
15. Spare collar.

For the most part, health is maintenance and prevention. You can correct the little things that go wrong with your dog, but for anything out of the ordinary, consult your veterinarian. You should have a relationship with him similar to that of your family doctor. Feel free to call him on certain matters concerning your dog; his general knowledge of diet, grooming, in fact all phases of your dog's life, will be most helpful. Also, he keeps accurate records and when you move to another area, he will gladly transfer his information to the next man.

Teach your dog not to bark excessively.

8

TRAINING & TRICKS

Now is the time to have fun with your puppy!

Up to this point we've been rather serious. It was necessary in order to be practical. You bought your puppy to enjoy it, and from here on, you will. You'll teach it to be a companion, a pal, do some tricks, maybe even a little protection work like barking on command. Dogs love to learn to do things that please you. Once taught, they will fetch a ball for you endlessly, carry your pocketbook while shopping or lug the Sunday paper for you with great pride.

Each breed of dog was originally bred for a specific purpose. It had a mission in life, whether hunting, herding, ratting or what. In most cases that instinct is still strongly present, giving the dog an intense desire to be useful. Like people, dogs suffer from boredom. When ignored and left out of the action, they soon develop bad habits. So include your dog in as many of your activities as possible. It will make him a much more healthy and balanced animal.

As dogs grow older, they become characters just as people do. They develop their little idiosyncrasies and amusing mannerisms. They become more definite in their likes and dislikes, what they will put up with and what they won't. A real character of a dog is amusing to be around. Maybe this is where we get the expression "putting on the dog."

When we use the word "training" in this chapter, we mean teaching your dog those things which make your relationship with him more close and workable, which make him adjust better to our modern society. It hardly seems possible that only a generation ago there were almost no

Start training your puppy early.

leash laws, that a dog could run free without getting into or causing any harm. But times have changed, the country has grown and now demands more of its dogs as it does of its people. And so training is an important part of the modern dog's happy existence.

He must learn to walk mannerly on a leash along the street, through crowds, among other dogs, and comport himself like a gentleman. If you have a happy, attractive, outgoing dog, he will make more friends and account for your meeting more new people than almost anything else you can do. Any dog can be taught manners, and it's up to you, his master, to do it, not only for your own convenience and peace of mind but for the safety of your dog as well as the respect of your neighbors.

But before you begin you must, as the old gag says, know more than the dog.

Don't laugh. Dogs are not the dumb animals many people think. They have their ways and methods. They can drive a novice trainer to the point where he's ready to pull his hair out in frustration. But there is always a solution.

The major solution is to start your training early! Start while the dog is still young and his personality still soft enough to be easily molded.

This is especially true of the large and giant-sized dogs. Their training can begin at three or four months of age. If you wait until seven or eight months of age, their size is so massive that it is extremely difficult for the owner to maneuver them properly through the various exercises. At four months, the dog doesn't resist his training but goes along with it. You must never be heavy-handed or overbearing with a young puppy, but rather coax him into sitting, heeling and the other steps which we shall

Be sure his collar is on correctly.

Heel!

soon discuss. All dogs should begin their formal obedience training at no later than five or six months of age.

What usually happens when you start early is that the young dog complies until he reaches about a year of age. Then he gets a mind of his own and goes through a period of stubbornness which will require that you be more forceful and let him know that you're still the boss. Every dog goes through this stage, and it is better to have the training well implanted before than try to do it during or after this period. He will have days when he does everything right and days when his mind is off somewhere in the daisies. Once this three-to-six-month period has passed, the mature dog begins to emerge. You have lost a puppy but gained a true, lifelong friend.

The purpose of obedience training is to make a companion dog. The commands that you will teach are *Heel, Sit, Stay, Lie Down,* and *Come.* All have a practical side that makes them useful in daily living with your dog.

When guests come for a friendly visit, how nice it is to tell your dog to "Lie down!" and have him oblige. Many people are timid, even afraid of dogs, but a well trained one gives them confidence and brings both you and the dog a flood of compliments.

On the other hand, nothing is worse than trying to balance a cocktail glass in your hand while a dog is climbing all over you. His master shouts at him but he has deaf ears. He gobbles up half the hors d'oeuvres, drools over the other half, then tries to sit in the lap of the best-dressed woman at the party.

Training is done by repetition, reward and praise. It utilizes voice, timing and a desire to please.

Your voice tells him what to do. The exercise is repeated over and over until the dog understands what is wanted. Each time he makes a mistake, you make a correction by a snap on the leash which in turn tightens his collar as a reminder. Each time he does it right, you reward him with verbal praise or a tidbit on special occasions. By the distinction between the jerk on the collar and your lavish praise, he learns what you want done. And because you are his master and the object of his love, he has a desire to please you. In some breeds, this is much stronger than others, but it is present in all puppies, which is another reason for starting young.

Every dog is different. You have to coax the shy dog, make firm demands on the bully and pep up the loafer. Be serious with the clown and firm against the obstinate. Be calm with the nervous dog and disguise your corrections from the skeptic. Study your dog's personality before you start and decide just what approach will help him the most.

Your training tools are simple: a six-foot, $\frac{1}{2}''$ or $\frac{5}{8}''$ leather leash and a choke chain collar for medium and large dogs, a six-foot light leather leash and rolled leather collar for the small dog and toy. Later you will want a 15- to 30-foot web leash or rope to teach your dog to come.

Practice every day for at least ten minutes. Try to make the lessons fun and appealing. If you can squeeze in two ten-minute sessions, one in the morning and one at night, it will be even better. Two short sessions daily are far more effective than one long one once a week. The dog will learn much faster. Always train before a meal, never after. Work in a spot where there are few distractions. You want to hold his attention just as completely as possible. Once you and the puppy have gotten the knack of it, you can and should practice where there are more distractions.

Be sure your collar is on correctly as shown on page 81. The chain will loosen each time after you snap the leash. The dog should always be on your left side, his head parallel to your left knee. Gather the leash in your right hand, letting it run through your left hand which remains down at your side and makes the corrections. Work on a loose leash.

When you give a command, always use the dog's name first to gain his attention. Example: "Laddie, SIT!" (The only exception to this rule is when you leave your dog for the STAY! command.) Don't use a lot of verbiage, just his name and the command—nothing else. Always be consistent in your commands, never deceive the dog.

Always give the dog a moment to respond. If he doesn't, then snap the lead for your correction, and follow it with verbal praise as the dog begins to do it.

The first command is "HEEL!"

With the dog at your left side, say in a loud, clear voice, "Laddie, HEEL!" Start walking forward briskly. If your dog does not follow, give him a light snap on the leash and praise him with "Good boy!" as he begins to come along. If he lunges ahead, pull back with a snap on the leash. Your left hand does all the work. If the dog lags behind or wanders to the side, repeat the command and snap the leash until he responds. Don't haul on the dog. Make your snap and let up. You should be able to hear the chain collar zip as you do it.

Second command is "SIT!"

While you are moving with your dog at heel, stop. As you stop, take up the slack in the leash in your right hand, put the fingers of your left hand on the dog's hip bones and say firmly, "Laddie, SIT!" At the same time, give a slight upward pull on the leash to raise the dog's head and push down on his rump. He will automatically sit beside you.

Already you have taught your dog two commands. Practice them over and over. Praise your dog as he follows along at heel position. Give him a pat on the side when you stop and push him into a sit. Practice also turning to the right and left. When you make a right-about turn, tell your dog to heel, then remind him with a snap on the leash. Praise him as he comes around, and pat the side of your leg to keep him close to you.

Sit!  Stay!

For a left or U-turn, push your right knee into the dog as you come about: if he's a small fellow, use your foot.

Remember to practice often but not so long that your puppy becomes confused. Try to make it all seem like fun, but keep it precise. Make sure he sits squarely beside you, not at an angle. Coax him, cajole him into it but make sure he does it.

The third command is "STAY!"

This most useful exercise is merely an extension of "SIT!" The object is for him to remain in a sitting position while you move around. While he is sitting beside you, put all the lead in your right hand, place the palm of your left hand in front of his nose and say firmly, "STAY!" without using his name. Take one step forward on your right foot, turn and face your dog. If he moves, push him back into a sitting position, repeating the command and using your right hand, palm facing him, to show him what is wanted. Wait a moment, then step back to his side.

As he learns, gradually begin to move farther away from him until you reach the full length of the leash. Begin returning to him via his left side so that you pass around behind him. Keep the leash to his right side

Lie down! with hand signal.

as you move and it won't become twisted. Once the dog has become proficient at this, use the 30-foot rope and move to the end of it. Let a full minute pass, then return to him.

The fourth command: "LIE DOWN!"

Also a most useful command, it is sometimes difficult to teach but your dog will grasp it if you are persistent. With your dog in a sitting position, bend down on your right knee, grasp the leash close to the snap in your right hand and say, "Laddie, LIE DOWN!" Pull down firmly with your right hand and at the same time press down on the dog's shoulders with your left hand. The small or medium-sized dog will go down easily; the large dog may resist. If he does, just simply wait him out

Lie down!

while maintaining pressure on his collar and shoulders until he finally sinks down. Praise him profusely when he does. Practice this until he goes down easily.

   To be really flashy at this, you want your dog to drop on raised hand signal. For this, put your dog in a sitting position, tell him to stay, take a step forward and face him just slightly to the right of center. With the lead in your left hand, let it sag in an arc until it hangs six inches off the floor. Get your dog's attention, raise your right hand like a policeman and say "Laddie, LIE DOWN!" At the same time, raise your right foot and stamp down on the leash. The result will be a downward snap similar to what you did while kneeling. If the dog resists, wait him out

87

Come!

again. With a little practice he will soon learn to drop on your command and raised arm, on and off leash; finally just your arm signal will do the trick.

Last, and probably the most important command of all, is teaching your dog to come when called.

For it, put your dog in a Sit-Stay position and with the 30-foot leash, move to the full length of it. Wait a few seconds, then call him happily. Say: "Laddie, COME!" Chances are he won't know what to do, so give a slight snap on the leash until he responds. As he begins to come toward you, praise him loudly and happily, at the same time reeling in the rope so he can't wander off to the side. When he reaches you, have him sit in front of you. This is one time it is good to offer a tidbit as a reward. Do it right from the beginning and his response will be consistently better. But give it to him only after he has come to a sitting position squarely in front of you.

Believe it or not, your dog is now well trained enough to enter obedience competition. Yes, you would need a few more commands, but not many. Before you consider that, however, be sure to practice in different places and under different conditions. When you take your dog for a walk, put him through his paces. Inside the car, make him lie down. Have him sit when a friend comes to visit. Use the training at every opportunity.

Once you feel very sure of your dog, try practicing off-leash. Better do it inside the house or apartment at first. Leave the leash on him and throw it loosely over your right shoulder. Then take it off altogether. Practice outside in a fenced area at first, a school yard perhaps. Finally, put him to the test and try him on a street. You can let him drag his leash at first.

Now for a few tricks so you can really boast about your pet.

One of the oldest that is always fun: Shake Hands. With your dog in a sitting position, face him at his level even if it means kneeling, and say, "SHAKE HANDS!" At the same time, take his paw and shake it. Afterwards reward him with a tidbit. With a little practice he will be doing it with either paw, although some dogs seem to be more right-handed than left, or vice-versa.

Shake hands!

Another cute trick is having your dog speak on command. It's not always an easy thing to teach; some dogs grasp it quickly, others never do. There are several ways of doing it. You can make your dog sit in front of you while you slowly reach out with your forefinger and tap his nose, at the same time hissing the command, "S-s-s-speak!" Repeated over and again, the dog soon begins to bark at you out of annoyance, whereupon you can praise him and have him barking every time you raise your finger. Another way is to tease the dog with a tidbit that he wants. You don't give it to him until he barks. Meanwhile, you tell him to "Speak!" and hold the tidbit between the extended forefinger and middle finger which becomes a signal when he responds.

Kids get great fun out of having their dog beg, and it's a simple thing to teach. Have your dog sit in a corner with carpet or a rug under him so he doesn't slip. Hold a tidbit slightly above his nose so he can smell it. As he follows it with his eyes, catch him under his forelegs with your other hand and raise him up. Hold him there a few seconds so he gets used to the sensation, then give him the tidbit. A little practice will have him doing it regularly. This trick is easy enough for the older dog but for a young puppy it is difficult because it requires a sense of balance. Wait until your dog is at least six months old before trying to teach him.

The easiest way to teach your dog to dance is to make him dance for his supper. Hold his food pan out of reach above him, and order "Dance!" After a time or two he will gladly rear on his hind legs for you.

"Catch!" is another game that can be taught with tidbits. All you have to do is have him sit in front of you about three feet distant and you toss pieces of his favorite tidbit to him. Arch them in the air so he can see them better. He may miss a few at first but he'll soon be shagging them like a centerfielder grabs fly balls.

"Roll Over!" is taught from the "Down" position. Simply have a tidbit in your hand and make a circular motion with it in front of the dog's nose while at the same time you roll him over with your free hand. Do it on a carpet or something soft so the dog finds the movement pleasant. Afterwards, you want to give him the tidbit of course.

A good series of tricks that is fun to teach your dog is *HOLD, CARRY* and *FETCH*. The first naturally leads to the second and the second to the third, and all are fun.

To teach "Hold!" use your dog's favorite toy or old sock knotted in the middle. Have him sit in front of you and wave the object in front of him. If he reaches out and takes it, tell him "Hold!" or "Hold it!" and praise him if he does. If he won't take it, open his mouth and slip it behind his fangs, close his mouth gently, telling him to "Hold it!" and

Speak!

tickling him under the chin to make certain he does. If he drops it, start over. No tidbit reward here, just good verbal praise when he does it.

You'll want to teach him to carry the object next, but make sure he knows "Hold it!" first. For this carrying bit, put a leash on him and with the object in his mouth, lead him around the house, then outside. Don't have him hold it too long, especially if it has any weight to it. Praise him afterwards so that he feels proud. Have him sit and let him give it to you on the command of "Give!"

The last step is to teach the dog to fetch the object and bring it to you. Start off by having the dog sit beside you with a short, light leash on. Toss the object he likes to carry about four to six feet away and tell him enthusiastically to "Fetch!" He will eagerly pounce on it and chances are, bring it back to you immediately. If he doesn't, you have the leash on him so you can coax him back. A little practice will soon have him fetching from considerable distances.

Retrievers of course are great at this sort of thing, but all dogs have a natural instinct to do it if they are encouraged and developed in the right manner.

Jumping through a hoop is a big game for most dogs. Some get so excited that they bark gaily. To teach this, simply hold the hoop in front of the dog a few inches off the ground at first and coax him to jump for

Teach your dog to ride in a car.

When you take your dog out of the car, be sure it is on a leash.

a tidbit. Say "Hup!" as he goes through, and give him a big cheer. You can raise it a little each time and soon he'll be springing through it for all he's worth.

One last point in regard to training. If you want to teach your dog to bark at strangers who come to the door, have a neighbor come and rattle the handle or make a few scratching sounds that the dog can hear. Just two or three times of this will have the dog on his toes and barking. This is not a wise thing to do if you have a large dog. As time passes, he may become more and more aggressive and one day you lose control of him, especially if someone innocently bursts into your home or apartment. A small dog may never be more than yappy, but a large dog tends to become more and more aggressive.

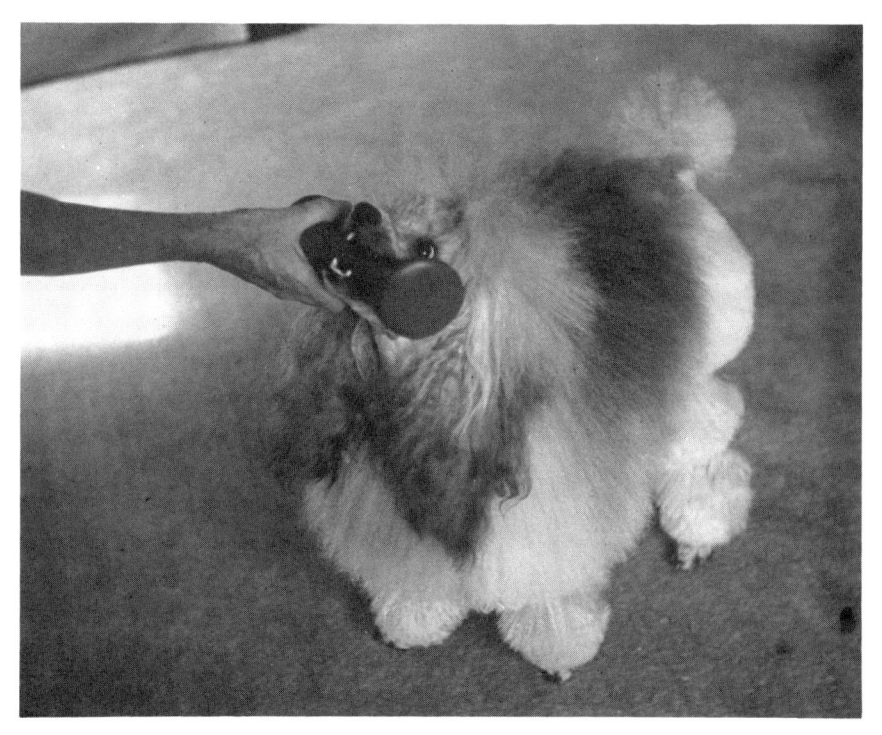

It's easy to teach your puppy to carry an object.

The American Kennel Club does not recommend the use of guard dogs in the home. They are one-man dogs, highly trained and always skillfully handled. When in use, they are accompanied by their master; when not in use, they are kenneled.

You can teach your dog with little or no effort to ride in the car and protect it for you. Simply take your dog with you when you go driving and leave him in the car when you run errands. Be sure to leave the windows open several inches, not enough for him to get out but enough for ample ventilation. Make a practice of always leaving the dog in the car. Ask a couple of your friends to walk up to the car. Tell them not to antagonize the dog, but merely to put their hand on the door handle as if to open it. When the dog starts to bark, they are to walk away. If the dog enjoys riding in the car and if you leave him in it each time you get out to run an errand, he will soon be guarding it with his life, regardless of his size.

9
GENERAL INFORMATION

When you bought your pedigreed dog you received an application for registration, or what is commonly called "papers." This means that your dog is purebred, has a proud lineage of ancestors, and is eligible to be registered with the American Kennel Club, the largest registry in the United States.

Don't lose these "papers." They are very difficult to replace. Fill them out, decide on a name for your dog and send them with the proper fee to the American Kennel Club. If the form is correct, you will receive in a month to six weeks' time a certificate of registration which bears your dog's official name and number. From then on, any time you compete with your dog or have reason to write to the AKC about him, be sure to use this number and official name.

Because your dog is purebred, he is eligible to participate in dog shows, obedience trials, field trials, even herding trials. Thousands of these events are held annually throughout the country. No matter where you live, there will be one or more nearby.

Dog shows are held outside in the summer and inside in the winter in armories, auditoriums and sporting arenas. The show consists of a series of competitions, each more difficult than the last. The winners of each class keep competing until best of each breed is determined; these in turn vie for best of the six group classifications—Sporting Dogs, Hounds, Working Dogs, Terriers, Toys and Non-sporting Dogs. These six winners then compete for the grand prize, *Best in Show*.

Obedience trials are usually held in conjunction with dog shows on an adjoining part of the grounds. Sometimes training clubs hold their

Dog shows are fun.

own special meets. All breeds of purebred dogs are welcome if they have had sufficient formal obedience training to be manageable. A well trained dog can earn four degrees which are officially added to the rear of his name: CD (Companion Dog), CDX (Companion Dog Excellent), UD (Utility Dog), and T (Tracking Dog). Each is more advanced than the other, hence more difficult. Obedience trials are fascinating to watch and exciting to participate in. A majority of the competitors are women.

Several different kinds of field trials are held throughout the country, mostly in rural areas because a lot of land is generally needed, and here men come to compete with their dogs. At bird dog trials for the pointing breeds—pointers, setters, Brittany Spaniels, German Shorthairs, Weimaraners, Vizslas, etc.—the handlers usually ride horseback. Beagle and Basset trials are run on rabbits and are so popular that there are trials somewhere in the country every weekend of the year.

Foxhound trials and Coonhound trials are held in rural areas, the latter sometimes at night. Retriever trials for Labradors, Chesapeakes, Goldens and other retrievers, take place across the country beside lakes, swamps, rivers and ocean bays. The spaniels—Springers and Cockers—have their field trials too, colorful events at which pheasants are flown and shot.

Herding meets for Border Collies and other breeds who tend sheep are held on a lesser scale across the country. And there are even several formal Beagle packs run from foot on weekends just to hear the merry baying.

Yes. There are a lot of things you can do with your dog!

To obtain a calendar of dog show events, write the American Kennel Club, 51 Madison Avenue, New York, N. Y. Or you can ask your veterinarian. He is knowledgeable in this area and can tell you who to call for further information. New faces are always welcome among dog people.

In any competition involving dogs, the procedure is a bit complicated and confusing until you become familiar with it. Before you enter your dog, it is best to go and take in an event involving whatever you happen to be interested in. Spend an afternoon at a dog show. See how your particular breed is prepared for the ring. Watch how dogs are handled, the pattern they follow inside the ring under judgment. Note the leashes, combs, brushes which are used to make the dogs look their best. Watch

At field trials, dogs point wild game.

the obedience ring and see how the dogs work, individually and in a group, what is required of them.

Buy a catalog and see how the numbers in it correspond to the exhibitor numbers in the book. The names and addresses of all owners who are showing will be listed in the back, thus giving you a chance to contact someone later if you wish.

The American Kennel Club issues licenses for two types of shows—sanctioned shows and matches. Sanctioned shows are the big important events which the professional handlers attend. Here competition is toughest, but you will see some magnificent dogs.

Match shows are more relaxed and fun. Amateurs bring their dogs so both they and their dogs can learn and gain experience. This is the the best place for you to start showing your dog if you want to try it. Ribbons and trophies are awarded.

As we mentioned earlier, almost every breed of dog has a national club, the address of which can be obtained through the AKC. If your breed does not have a club near you, there will certainly be an all-breed club nearby, or an obedience club. Among the many activities that they sponsor, besides shows, are guest lecturers, dog films, dog seminars, training and grooming and judging clinics. You will find them crammed with valuable information and be among enthusiastic, like-minded people.

In case you are having trouble training your dog, there are several hundred obedience training clubs and organizations across the country where dogs and their owners go to group classes once a week. Again, you can ask your veterinarian or write to the Gaines Dog Research Center, 250 Park Avenue, New York, N. Y. for a free list of such classes in your locality.

Also, there are several magazines devoted to dogs. Each breed that is large enough to have a national club has some sort of monthly periodical. Some of them are very fine magazines, with valuable information and the latest news about that particular breed. The larger, all-breed magazines cover dogs and dog supplies on a larger scale, many giving show and field trial results.

Obedience trials are a challenge for you and your dog.

When traveling with your dog, make sure you have its license, as well as rabies and identification tags.

10
TRAVELING WITH YOUR DOG

A word on traveling with your dog.

Once you become attached to your pal and the relation grows stronger through the years, you will want to take him with you on trips. There is no reason why he can't go along providing you do a little planning.

First off, you should teach your puppy to ride in the car early in life so he learns to enjoy it and not become sick. Almost every dog, if introduced to riding properly, ends up loving it. Before you ever take him any place, sit in the car with him a few times. Let him smell it, see its reflections, give him a tidbit. Start the motor the second or third time and let the car just roll forward.

When he goes for his first ride, hold him in your lap while someone else drives. Make it a short spin, and keep talking to him so he doesn't lose confidence. Have the window open so he gets a breeze and can also enjoy some smells. Dogs love to ride with their heads out of the window, the breezes flapping their ears. It is not particularly good for them. Bits of trash or bugs can get in their eyes, but still it does seem to keep them from getting car sick. If your dog drools or vomits after all this training, then the best thing to do is have your veterinarian give you some pills which will settle the dog's stomach when he goes on a long ride. Take them with you on trips.

If you own a station wagon, the back is ideal for the dog's riding area. There are handy barriers which you can put up just behind the back seat. Made of wire, they keep the dog from jumping back and forth and annoying the driver; they are also easily seen through and can be removed with little effort.

Most people who go to shows or field trials with their dogs transport them in wire cages made to fit the back of the station wagon. Each dog has his own compartment and cannot be annoyed by any other one. It is the generally accepted way of carrying all competitive dogs except the very large ones. Your car is protected and so is the dog.

If you have a passenger car, the best place for the dog is the back seat. Put down a terrycloth towel or canvas for protection, roll down a window partway so he gets plenty of air but can't jump out. He will travel contented and much better than in the trunk. So many accidents and deaths have occurred to dogs carried in trunks that it is impossible to recommend this as anything but a last resort. There is a trunk ventilator that can be attached and theoretically supplies plenty of fresh air, but between the poison gas fumes and the heat that comes from standing or even riding in the sun, it just isn't worth the risk if you love your dog.

When you plan to take your dog traveling, it's wise to include his own food so you won't have to change brands along the way. This can cause diarrhea which is bad enough without being in a car. If you go just for a day or two, you may want to include some local water too, rather than give him water from the area which you are visiting. This will cut down on the chances of an upset stomach.

Have his collar on his neck and make sure it includes his license, rabies tag and identification tag. You also want a good strong leash and if he is used to wearing a sweater at home, take one along just in case the weather changes.

Some motels and hotels refuse to accept dogs while others welcome them with open arms. For a handy list of those which accept dogs, send twenty-five cents to the Gaines Dog Research Center, 250 Park Avenue, New York, N. Y. for a copy of "Touring with Towser," the bible for travelers with dogs.

If you cross state lines, it will be wise to have your veterinarian give you a health certificate. Many states require this along with a rabies vaccine injection. You may never be stopped for that specific reason, but you might be for something else and in the process be asked for these papers. Dog regulations differ from state to state, but these two items will cover you just about anywhere you go except Hawaii which has a quarantine, so taking your dog there unless you planned to stay a while would not be worthwhile.

As you drive through a national park, don't stop and open the door to let your dog have a nice carefree run. There are special laws and strict rules against this. Ask the park supervisor about it first.

For the small dog, a carrying case is very handy.

Once again, whenever you leave your dog in the car, be sure you park in the shade and leave the windows slightly open for ventilation. Hot sun on the metal top and glass windows will turn it into a furnace that will suffocate him to death. Also, don't tie the dog inside the car. He can easily hang himself.

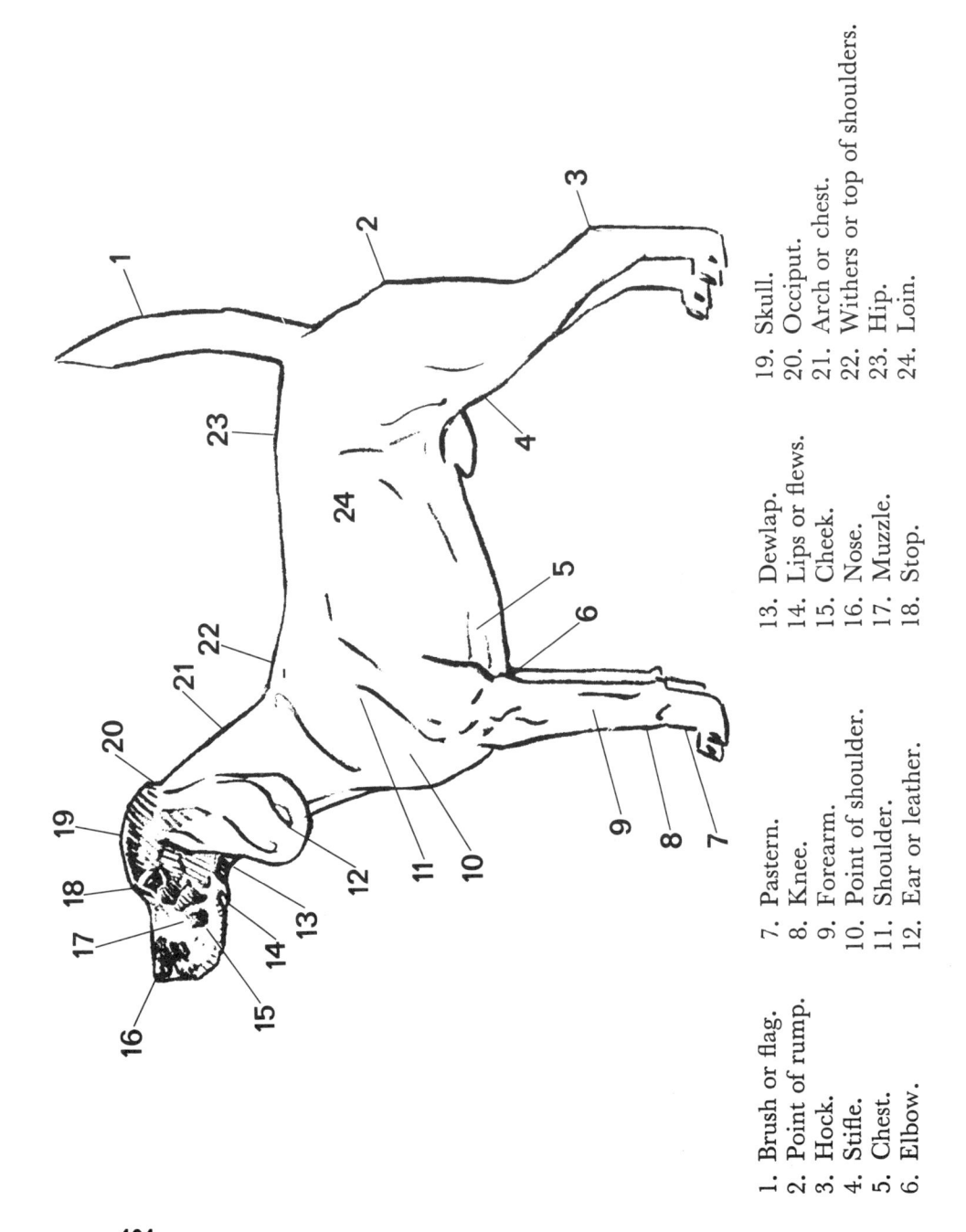

1. Brush or flag.
2. Point of rump.
3. Hock.
4. Stifle.
5. Chest.
6. Elbow.
7. Pastern.
8. Knee.
9. Forearm.
10. Point of shoulder.
11. Shoulder.
12. Ear or leather.
13. Dewlap.
14. Lips or flews.
15. Cheek.
16. Nose.
17. Muzzle.
18. Stop.
19. Skull.
20. Occiput.
21. Arch or chest.
22. Withers or top of shoulders.
23. Hip.
24. Loin.

When you travel by plane with your dog it is possible to take him with you, but only small dogs and puppies are usually permitted in the passenger compartments, and then they must be in carry cases. Otherwise, he will have to travel in the baggage compartment in a special airlines' dog crate. These are inexpensive and nicely constructed.

When you find it necessary to ship your dog from one point to another, air travel is of course by far the fastest. Most companies have their own set of rules, and the dog will need to have a health certificate and possibly a vaccination. Call the airline that you plan to use first and they will gladly supply this information. They will not accept a dog unless its shipping papers are in order.

For short distances you may use the railroad for shipping. The same rules apply if he crosses state lines.

Sending or traveling with your dog abroad is more complicated, but it can be done quite easily except for those countries which have quarantine. These are England, Sweden, Denmark and Finland. Most all require health certificates and some insist that a rabies inoculation has been given six months prior to entry. The dog can be flown to his destination or sent by steamship, most of which have kennels aboard.

Don't let your dog run loose!

HOW YOUR DOG LEARNS

REPETITION — This means practicing over and over with your dog whatever you are trying to teach him until he understands it. It also means being consistent and requiring that he do it under all circumstances.

PRAISE — This is the reward he receives for doing a job correctly, especially in the beginning. It is a pat of the flank or a happily spoken "Good boy!" or a hug or any gesture he particularly likes.

CORRECTION — This is the discipline he receives through your tug on the collar or tone of voice or spanking if necessary. It is particularly through the difference between praise and correction that your dog learns.

TIMING — After you give a command, always allow your dog an instant to respond before making a correction.

VOICE — Your dog soon learns to know exactly what kind of person you are and how much is expected of him by the tone of your voice.

DESIRE TO PLEASE — The closer friend you make of your dog, the stronger will be his desire to please you and the easier he will be to train.

INDEX

abroad, traveling with your dog, 105
airplane, traveling by, 105
auto accidents, 72
"bark," 78, 93
basket, wicker, 52
bathing, 48–49
bee stings, 74
"beg," 90
bitch, 22
    brood, 25
bleeding,
    control of, 72
    use of tourniquet, 72
body, parts of, 104
boots for puppies, 15
breeding, 22–23
britches, doggy, 20
"burgers," 30
burns, 69
care and grooming, 43 ff.
    bathing, 48–49
    clipping nails, 45
    ears, 45
    eyes, 43–44
    grooming coat, 46
"carry," 90
cars, riding in, 101–103
"catch," 90
chain collar, 11
charcoal biscuit, 34
chewing, how to discourage, 9
children and puppies, 5
clubs,
    national, 97
    obedience training, 95–96
coat,
    care of, 47
    changing color, 25
collar,
    chain, 11
    in training, 83
    leather, 11
    rolled, 11
    selecting, 11
"come," 88
commercially prepared foods, 28
crying, how to soothe, 7
cuts, 72
"dance," 90
dangers to puppies' health, 7–8
degrees awarded at obedience trials, 96
disciplining, 9–14
    see also training and tricks

diseases, 8
    distemper, 63
    hepatitis, 63
    insects as cause of, 58–60
    leptospirosis, 63
    signs of, 58–61
    skin, 60
    worms, 60–63
distemper, 63
dog fights, 72
dog shows, 95–96
    matches, 96
    sanctioned shows, 97
door, come-go, 56
ears,
    care of, 45
    types of, 45
eczema,
    dry, 60
    wet, 60
eyes, checking, 43–44
feces, cleaning up, 41
feeding, 27 ff.
    amounts of food, 31
    charcoal biscuit, 34
    commercially prepared foods, 28
    leftovers, 28
    mixed feeding, 28
    nutrition, 28–29
    overfeeding, 32
    proper utensils for, 11, 34
    raised feeder, 34
    times, 27–28
    unusual foods, 34
    water, 34
feet, 45
    clipping toenails, 45
"fetch," 92
field trials, 96–97
fights, see dog fights
first aid, 66 ff.
    administering medication, 65, 67
    auto accidents, 72
    bee stings, 74
    burns, 69
    control of bleeding, 72
    cuts and scratches, 72
    dog fights, 72
    first aid kit, 77
    fractures, 69
    inducing dog to vomit, 70–71
    poisoning, 71
    preventive measures, 66
    simple muzzle, 66, 68

    snake bites, 74
    splint, 69–70
    sprains, 69
    swallowing foreign objects, 70–71
    tourniquet, 72
first aid kit, 77
fleas, control of, 58–60
food,
    "burgers," 30
    dry, 28
    kibble, 28–29
    leftovers, 28
    meat, cooked, 28
    unusual, 34
foreign objects, swallowing, 70
fractures, 69
general information, 95 ff.
gestation period, 26
grooming, 46
    Poodle, 48
growth patterns, 22–25
handling puppy correctly, 5
    teaching children about, 5
health, 7–8, 58 ff.
    administering medication, 65
    care and grooming, 43 ff.
    danger to puppies', 7–8
    diseases, 8, 58–63
    feeding, 27 ff.
    female puppy's season, 22-23
    first aid, 66 ff.
    fleas, control of, 58–60
    insects, as a hazard to, 58–60
    measuring puppy's height, 24
    medicines, 21
    permanent shots to protect, 8
    shedding coat, 25
    signs of sickness, 58
    skin diseases, 60
    teeth, 43
    temperature taking, 65
    ticks, control of, 58–60
    ways to protect, 15
    weighing puppy, 64
    worms, 60–63
heartworms, 60, 62
"heel," 83, 84
height, measuring dog's 24
hepatitis, 63

107

"hold," 90
home, bringing puppy to, 5
hookworms, 60
housebreaking, 16, 18, 36 ff.
  accidents, 38, 41
  paper training, 36
  taking puppy outside, 38
  trolley, use of, 40
  when to start, 36
housing, 51 ff.
  basket, 52
  cellar, 51
  crate, 51
  dog house, 51–54
  fencing, 52
  outdoor, 51
  run, 52, 54–55
how your dog learns, 106
inoculations, 8
insects,
  as a hazard to health, 58–60
  fleas, 58–60
  ticks, 58–60
jumping through a hoop, 92
kibble, 28–29
leash,
  getting puppy used to, 11
  in training, 13
  selecting, 11
  traffic, 11
  web-type, 11, 83
leather collar, 11
leftovers, feeding, 28
license for puppy, 25
"lie down," 86
lifting puppy correctly, 5
liquid medication, administering, 67
Lord Byron's Epitaph for His Dog Buried at Newstead Abbey, 1808, 2
male puppy, castrating, 25
matches, 97
measuring dog's height, 24
meat, 28
medicine for puppy, 21
  liquid, 67
  pills, 67
mischief, puppy getting into, 5
mixed feeding, 28
"Motto for a Dog House," 51
muzzle, use of in first aid, 66, 68

nails, clipping, 45
name,
  on registration papers, 21, 95
  selecting, 21
  teaching to puppy, 21
nutrition, 32
obedience trials, 95–96
  degrees awarded at, 96
overfeeding, 32
pacifiers, 33
paper training, 36
pills,
  administering, 65
  taken during female's season, 22
playpen for puppy, 15
poisoning, 71
Poodle, grooming, 48
profile of a dog, 104
protective nature of puppy, 13
railroad, traveling by, 105
raincoats for puppies, 15
raised feeder, 34
registration papers, 21, 95
rolled collar, 11
"roll over," 90
roundworm, 60
run, fenced, 52, 54–55
  fencing, 54
  trolley, 40
sanctioned shows, 98
season, female puppies', 22
  breeding during, 22–23
  doggy britches, 20
  pills taken during, 22
  spaying, 23
"shake hands," 89
shedding, 25
shots, permanent, 8
shows, dog, *see* dog shows
sickness, signs of, 58
"sit," 84
skin diseases, 60
sleeping place, 7
snake bites, 74
socializing with dog, 13
spaying female puppy, 23
"speak," 90
splint, 69–70
sprains, 69
Standard, official, 26
"stay," 85
stud dog, 26

sweaters for puppies, 15
tapeworms, 60
tartar on teeth, 43
tattooing for identification, 25
teeth,
  care of, 43
  loosing baby, 22
  tartar on, 43
temperature taking, 65
ticks, control of, 58–60
tools to clean puppy's run, 41
tourniquet, 72
toys for puppy, 9
training, 79 ff.
  "bark," 78, 93
  "come," 88
  commands used for, 83
  "heel," 83, 84
  "lie down," 86
  methods of general, 84
  riding in a car, 94
  "sit," 84
  "stay," 85
  when to start, 81
traveling with your dog, 101 ff.
  abroad, 105
  by car, 101–103
  by plane, 105
  by railroad, 105
  dog regulations, 102, 105
  hotels and motels, 102
  in wire cages, 102
trials,
  field, 96–97
  obedience, 95–96
tricks, 89–93
trolley line, 40
tug of war, 9
veterinarian, selecting a, 7
virus diseases, 65
vomiting, inducing, 70–71
water, importance of, 32
weighing, 64
whipworms, 62
wire crate,
  as playpen, 7, 51
  for traveling, 102
worms, 60–63
  heartworms, 60
  hookworms, 60, 62
  roundworms, 60
  tapeworms, 60
  treatment of, 63